Write On! How To Make Writing a Pleasurable Pastime

In *Write On!* Irene Hannigan helps dispel the loneliness of writing with friendly, commonsense advice on keeping a writing practice, on writing as process, and on the importance of suspending the internal critic to keep things fluent. Through the force of her charming and personable style, Hannigan's book becomes a companion—something every writer, whether s/he knows it or not, is in great need of.

— **Tom Daley, Creative Writing Instructor**

Carry a notebook. Record thoughts and observations. Write every day. Play with words. Don't censor. Reread what you write. Rewrite. Writing is a process, Irene Hannigan reminds the fledgling writer. *Write On!* is an easy to read, easy to follow recipe for anyone who has ever wanted to write.

— **Beverly Beckham, Boston Globe Columnist**

Writing should be as natural an act as breathing. *Write On!* is the result of a lifelong teacher's belief that writing is essential to our well-being. You will not find a better writing coach. With the simple directness of a great teacher Irene Hannigan will not only enable you to write but inspire you to start.

— **Ib Bellew, Publisher**

Write On! is an essential guidebook for both novice and experienced writers. It is filled with practical and inspiring suggestions for both sustaining your writing—as well as your writing life.

— **Georgia Heard, author of** *The Woman In This Poem: Women's Voices in Poetry*

Irene Hannigan offers a myriad of ways in which ordinary people can enrich their lives by putting some of their ideas and experiences on paper. For nearly all of us the goal wouldn't be to make a living as an "author" but to find a voice as a writer. *Write On!* is a book to cherish.

— **Jim O'Brien, Freelance Editor**

Write On!

How To Make Writing
A Pleasurable Pastime

Irene Hannigan

Cover design and illustrations
Laura Schreiber

Cover and illustrations: Laura Schreiber
Production and interior design: Kristine Rencs

For You

CONTENTS

ACKNOWLEDGEMENTS

I am grateful to Polly Attwood, Carol Birdsall, Jenn Eisenheim, Kristen Gobiel, and Martha Regan who suggested twenty years ago that I start a writing group. Linda Levin, Edie Lipinski, Penny Staples, Kitsy Rothermel, and Mary Yardley, who seamlessly became active members several years later, have greatly enhanced our group. My friend Roberta Messina helped me to set attainable goals during the initial stages of my writing. She gently held me accountable for meeting them and boosted my spirits when I needed encouragement. Cheryl Melody Baskin, Chris Farrow-Noble, and the late Jan Slepian never doubted that I had a manuscript within me. Our ongoing conversations about writing were invaluable in helping me to clarify my ideas and to believe in myself.

Ib Bellew appreciated my perspective about the value of writing as a satisfying pastime. He also urged me to conceptualize my project as a "how-to" book that would potentially help others. Rich Skalstad's kind words validated the merit of my work and his substantive feedback enabled me to make significant revisions.

Tom Daley and Jessie Brown have been inspirational teachers. They have broadened my writing repertoire to include memoir and poetry. Their thoughtful and insightful advice has enabled me to keep growing as a writer. I am thankful for the opportunities I have had to offer writing study groups at the Osher Lifelong Learning Institute at Tufts University under the leadership of David Fechtor. I have learned a great deal from the participants with whom I have worked and have appreciated their willingness to experiment with ideas and to offer feedback.

Barbara DeWolfe was an unwavering supporter of my project from the very start. She read early drafts, tried out many of the ideas, and convinced me of the value of my project. When I was looking for a copy editor, she volunteered to help me. I am grateful for her dedication and commitment to making my work the best it could be. I am indebted to Laura Schreiber who, despite her busy life as an illustrator and graphic designer, assured me that she would have time to create both a cover for my book as well as illustrations for each chapter. She couldn't have done a more perfect job. I was extremely fortunate to work with Kristine Rencs, who skillfully worked out all the logistics involved in publication. Her thoughtful questions and her attention to detail helped me realize the vision I had for my book.

And finally, many thanks to the two loves of my life—my husband Bob and my son Ted. They understand my quirky ways and receive my gifts of words with loving appreciation.

INTRODUCTION

For most of my adult life, I have been masquerading as a writer. As a teacher, staff developer, curriculum specialist, parent, and elementary school principal, I have always found that writing played a significant role in my life. I can't imagine a day without writing in a notebook I always have tucked in my pocket or purse. Once a week, my journal calls to me and I cherish the time to have a longer conversation with myself. I also attend a monthly writing group that I started twenty years ago.

I enjoy using writing to capture and to reflect on moments in my personal and professional life. It serves as a tool to help me think through problems and to explore solutions. I appreciate how writing helps me to be more observant of my surroundings. The thoughts and ideas I have, with my pen in hand, are always a source of discovery and often amusement. Especially when I was a working parent, I also came to appreciate that writing was an excellent way to make the time I needed to be in touch with myself. The sense of calm that comes over me as I write is always restorative and brings me much satisfaction. It is a pleasurable pastime and I feel fortunate that I have the luxury of not having to make a living from my writing.

Still, I do have two books to my credit and a number of articles that have been published in educational journals and teaching magazines. The articles and books materialized only after I had made writing a regular pastime. While seeing the results of my thinking in printed form is momentarily uplifting, publishing is never my ultimate goal. I write primarily for myself.

Write On! How to Make Writing a Pleasurable Pastime is a book intended to meet the needs of those of us who have this desire. Perhaps that is why you picked up this book. As you flipped through it, you had a feeling that it was significantly different from other books in the writing section of your favorite bookstore or library, such as—*Writing Your First Novel, You've Got a Book in You, Writing Fantasy and Science Fiction,* and *Getting Published.* For those of us who are just getting started, such books can be overwhelming.

Write On! however, is a book that fills a niche that has been ignored in the many books that have been written about writing. It is the kind of book I wish I could have found when I needed information about how to start and sustain a regular practice. While I had found bits and pieces of advice in a few books, I would have appreciated just one book aimed at a regular person like me—a book that I could read from cover to cover. *Write On!* is that kind of book. My goal is to offer concrete strategies that will enable you to explore what's involved in the writing process. Written in a conversational and user-friendly style, this book invites your participation, with your pen in hand, so let's get started!

Ilene Hannigan

Chapter One

What's the Point of Writing and Who Cares?

Free writing is the easiest way to get words on paper and the best all-around practice in writing I know.
—**Peter Elbow**

Admit it. If you've picked up this book, then you want to write. You may not know exactly why you want to write or even what you want to write about, but the idea is an appealing one. You may have occasionally turned to writing to help you think through solutions to problems. You may have used writing to vent your emotions after a crisis at home or at work. Perhaps you've even tried to capture in words a vacation memory and, upon reading it several years later, are so glad that you did.

You probably have more than a few partially filled blank books in your possession and yet you can't resist picking up just one more that catches your eye. *Maybe this is the journal I'm going to be comfortable writing in day after day*, you think to yourself as if a fancy journal possesses some hidden magic. Unfortunately, it does not. What is true, however, is that writing is a *process* that needs to be experienced in order to be understood, which is what this chapter is all about. This process takes time and it is time well spent for very personal reasons. It is about finding ideas to write about. It is about composing and drafting. It is about giving yourself permission to write for yourself without any further delay. It is about writing for an audience and that audience is YOU. Learning just a few strategies will enable you to write on a regular basis and to establish the habit of writing.

I still remember the discussion at the first meeting of my writing group. We had gathered together in my living room one summer morning in July, brimming over with our best intentions of making the upcoming summer one during which we would write on a regular basis. After all, most of us were teachers who were committed to helping our students become better writers. We knew that we needed to write if we were going to be able to teach our students. We also had a hunch that the pastime of writing was intrinsically satisfying. Our meeting began with a humorous "show and tell" that I would replicate at the start of every writing workshop or course I have ever offered to individuals from diverse backgrounds. It proved to me that teachers are not the only folks attracted to the potential promise of making writing a part of their lives.

"Just look at this assortment of books," Jenn exclaimed as one journal after another came tumbling out of her tote bag. "I especially love this one," she said holding up one with a marbleized cover that she couldn't resist purchasing. She was an art teacher who, during the past school year, had marbled paper with her students as part of a bookbinding project. Indeed all of her journals were lovely.

It was Martha's turn next. She also had a significant stash of blank books of all sizes. "It doesn't necessarily matter to me what the cover looks like," she said. "I'm attracted to ones that have quotes interspersed throughout. I thought the quotes would give me an idea of what to write about." She paused a bit before adding, deadpan, "Doesn't really work, though. It feels like too much of an assignment."

"I'm committed to journals that don't have a spiral binding," said Kristen in her matter-of-fact way before adding, "I'm left-handed. I like a journal that lies flat. I don't like battling with the binding." As the only other leftie in the group, I immediately understood what Kristen meant. It also explained why I rarely ever used the journals that I had received as gifts from friends. You have to buy one that just feels right for you.

It was then practical Polly's turn. "Well, for me the best kind of notebook is just the plain old spiral kind," she said with confidence holding up one with a bright red cover—the kind that you can pick up in any drug store—the kind that we always use in school. "Now don't get me wrong," she continued. "I have plenty of beautiful ones that have been given to me by friends but they're too lovely to use—intimidating maybe." Polly's words resonated with me. I could tell that the other members in our group felt she had a point. She was always so sensible.

One by one, we all commented about our choices of blank books, somewhat embarrassed by the fact that so many were only partially filled.

We continued to debate the merits of lined pages vs. blank pages. We shared opinions about the size and thickness. We even pooled our information about where we had found the best buys. We also talked about whether we preferred writing by hand or on our beloved computers. Ultimately, we realized that we were skillfully skirting the point of why we had gathered together on that lovely summer morning. Fortunately, we didn't begin to talk about our choice of pens! If this sounds familiar, then you know that you are not alone. Wouldn't it be wonderful if we could make writing a part of our lives simply by purchasing the correct journal or notebook or pen? But it's not going to happen and you already know that. That's why you've picked up this book.

The way to begin to establish the writing habit and, most importantly, how to sustain it is to accept the fact that writing is a *process*. The neat and tidy finished products—the publications that we are drawn to as readers— are the result of a *writing process* that takes a great deal of time and effort. But we don't *see* the initial stages of how professional writers identify a subject that is worth writing about. We don't *see* the painstaking false starts of the picture books we share with our children or the novels we read. We don't *realize* how many drafts preceded the articles we enjoy in our favorite magazines or the op-ed pieces in the newspaper that capture so clearly what we are thinking. Even a Hallmark greeting card has undergone many revisions before we find it on the shelf in the local card shop. Final publications are the result of a messy writing process that is hidden from view.

Still, when we sit down to write, we often think that we are instantly going to produce a quality product. How often have we labored over a note of condolence to a colleague or even a thank you note to a friend when we couldn't find adequate words in a published greeting card? We think we can do better and we try. But we often give up in frustration after just a short period of time. *Everyone else must be able to do it we say to ourselves. If I can't even compose a note that says what I really mean, how can I imagine ever writing anything more complicated?* The fact is that writing is a process that requires considerable time and effort and skill.

We need to give up the idea that producing a finished product each time we sit down to write is a realistic goal. Rather, we need to understand that writing is a process of thinking and that takes time. Peter Elbow, in his book *Writing With Power*, was one of the first writers to promote the idea of *free writing* as a way to experience the writing process as a tool for thinking. By placing our pen on a piece of paper and simply allowing our thoughts to come out, we give ourselves the opportunity to inspect our thoughts visually. Free writing on a regular basis enables us to experience what it feels like to write. We don't have to wait patiently for inspiration or for a good idea or even for a practical reason to write. All we have to do is simply write whatever we are thinking. We can experience what it feels like to let one word follow the next, and soon we discover that we have a sentence. Our brain will continue to be engaged with our pen and more words will make more sentences, more thoughts—our thoughts. After just five minutes, we can count up our words and sentences and say that we have been writing. It is a very freeing experience, especially for those of us who dreaded writing assignments in school and at work.

Although writing in this way may initially seem "pointless" because we have no finished product in the traditional sense, free writing does produce a practical product. Over time we have a notebook filled with pages of writing that we have created by listening to ourselves and documenting what we hear ourselves thinking. We can take pleasure in how many times we have written during the course of a week or month, providing we remember to date each entry. Indicating the time of day that we write will, over time, offer insight into possible patterns of our behavior. The place we choose to write will also offer useful information. Our product is for our eyes only, which is as it should be. After all, we are just getting started and we are our primary audience. We are no longer talking about writing or wishing we were writing. We are doing it and we have evidence in our notebook.

Freed from the pressure to find a perfect topic, we are procrastinators no longer. We appreciate the fact that all we have to do is to sit down with our notebook and keep our pen moving across the page. We might even consider this a new hobby which requires no special equipment or expertise. Five or ten minutes is a manageable amount of time for most of us if we decide to make it a priority. If we do it regularly enough, we start to trust that the words will come. We experience what it feels like to write. Our first goal is to just start writing *something*.

In our fast-paced, often frenetic and plugged-in technological world, the simple act of writing in this manner slows us down and forces us to make time for ourselves. Without any preconceived notion of what we are going to write, ideas worth thinking about surface and we're often pleasantly surprised about what emerges. Once we've made the commitment to ourselves to write, we start paying better attention to the people we encounter throughout our day and the situations in which we find ourselves. We discover that writing can help us capture and reflect on special moments we want to remember. It helps us to think through decisions and to solve problems. We make unexpected discoveries and often humorous insights. We discover that the writing soothes and centers us as we start to lead our lives with observant eyes, an open heart, and a reflective mind.

Writing for even five minutes never fails to produce a sense of calm within me. In fact, when I'm facilitating a meeting at work, having participants do a five-minute "free write" serves a useful purpose for them as well as for me. Here's an example of one of mine:

My forty minute commute this afternoon paled in comparison to the additional twenty minutes I spent in a very long line trying to get into the parking lot of the school where my meeting was. What a crazy situation for everyone involved but my heart really goes out to the principal who was directing traffic and teachers who were on dismissal duty. I wonder if this is a daily occurrence. I know I need do this free write right now to get myself ready for our meeting and I imagine the teachers will feel the same way. Even the teachers who were not "on duty" have had a busy day working with their students. They're tired and they need to switch gears.

Unloading on paper the difficulties participants may have had during their workday is a useful way for them to effectively transition to our meeting. Others, who may be preoccupied with a problem, appreciate the opportunity to let go of it on paper so they can be truly present for the meeting. Taking a few moments to unload our burdens, if only temporarily, causes us to realize how useful writing can be for ourselves and how easy it is to do. When that revelation occurs, then the motivation to find the time to write follows.

Free writing holds many benefits in addition to getting some words down on a sheet of paper quickly. Writing fast means that the critic that most of us have sitting on our shoulder will not have sufficient time to evaluate what we're writing. We also can't worry about what we're writing, since our task is to string one word after another as the words tumble out of our head and onto the page. There's no need to worry about whether the words are good enough, because how good can they be if we're not agonizing over each and every one? We're just getting on with the task of writing.

Another benefit, which is important for those of us who want to make writing a regular part of our lives, is that we can do it even when we don't feel inspired. What we write or where we write or for how long doesn't matter. Establishing a sustainable habit with this easy practice will boost our confidence.

A third benefit is that free writing often helps us to think of topics to write about. As soon as we put our pen to paper, our mind can't help but free associate. One idea leads to another. Suddenly we realize that we indeed have ideas. Best of all, they come from within us, unlike writing prompts that seem more like assignments. In addition, if we are organized enough to designate a specific time to write, we realize that ideas have been subconsciously percolating and start to emerge. When we find that ideas occur to us while we're taking our morning shower or an evening walk around our neighborhood, we have reached an important milestone in understanding the writing process. Topics are all around us. Our experiences can be a potential source of material and our lives may be more interesting than we once thought. Even though the free write is disjointed, seeing what we've been thinking about is illuminating. We give ourselves credit for having ideas.

Finally, free writing reinforces the idea that writing is all about thinking. The practice provides an opportunity for us to inspect our thinking. Unlike talking, our words don't disappear. Although what we see may not be exactly what we meant to say, free writing gives us the opportunity to keep tinkering with those thoughts that seem more compelling and worth further development. For this reason making time to periodically look back at what we've written is important. We need to search for patterns in our thinking or surprising thoughts that we were unaware we had. Who knows what we will uncover and discover in the process? If we keep to a five or ten minute free writing routine, the task of rereading will be a manageable one. If we write too much, it will take up more time than we realistically have. Rereading what we've written is another important part of the writing process.

This leads us to another strategy, a variation of free writing called the directed free write which is an opportunity for us to generate questions that we would like to think about more deeply. Putting an idea in the form of a question allows us to focus on a particular issue with intention. Unlike many books on writing that offer questions for writers, crafting our own questions is more meaningful. We are more likely to have a genuine desire to write on a topic that arises from our own thinking. Coming up with our own ideas is part of the writing process and this takes practice.

Directed free writes are especially useful if we plan to use writing as a way to help us achieve a balance between our personal and professional lives. I would not have been able to do my job as an elementary school principal if I had not kept an appointment with myself to write on a regular basis. I wrote about the staff meetings that had gone well, as well as the ones that had left me with a knot in my stomach. I wrote about the funny experiences I had with some children and the heartbreaking conversations I had with others. I sorted through my feelings about how to deal with directives coming from supervisors, as well as challenging requests from teachers and parents. My writing helped me to begin to address these issues. It became a useful tool that helped me slow down and reflect on my work life. It brought to me a sense of calm and well-being that gave me the confidence I needed to be able to move on. Completing a notebook of free writes or directed free writes over time provided a "product" that gave me a significant feeling of accomplishment.

Sometimes though, when we reread our free writes, we become discouraged when we notice how long some of our sentences are. When we remember that writing is a process that entails many false starts, we understand that a long, involved, convoluted sentence is a sign that we're not quite sure what we're trying to say—yet. Once we realize that what we are reading is a draft, we become less critical. When we accept the fact that many of our sentences are not going to emerge with uniform clarity, we appreciate that what we have written still holds promise of insights not yet uncovered. This discovery becomes a very compelling reason to continue to write. Free writing serves so many different purposes, not surprisingly, even for me as I was writing this chapter:

> I think I should mention the different subjects that often come off my pen depending upon the time of day I choose to write. During tonight's evening walk around the neighborhood I couldn't help but think about chapter one and whether or not I should include a couple of my own free-writes in the text as examples. Even though I do believe my words are for my eyes only maybe readers of this book would like to see a sample. I know that many of my morning free writes often have to do with how I'm planning to spend the day. Since retirement I've

had the luxury to have an entire day stretch out before me to fill with whatever I have on my own personal agenda. Some days are busier than others and I so love the control I have over my time. How different my free writes were when I was working. They served a different purpose.

Are you starting to warm up to the idea of what the point of writing might be for you personally? Can you see the wisdom of considering yourself as your audience? What if you chose one of your least precious blank books to accompany you on your reading of this book? I say "least precious" because I know how long it took me to eventually use one of my beautiful journals. If you're like Polly or me, you'll probably feel more comfortable with a plain spiral- bound notebook that you can pick up at any drug store. Write today's date at the top of the first page and for five minutes stop reading and start writing. Put your pen on the page and keep your hand moving. Let the words that are floating around in your head flow through your pen and onto the page where you will eventually be able to inspect them, but don't stop to reread what you've written now. Keep your hand moving. Write words or phrases. Write sentences if you wish, but be prepared for the possibility that some of them will be incomplete sentences while others will be run-ons. No one is judging. No one will even see what you've written. You are writing for yourself. Lower your expectations for now. Just give it a try. After five minutes, take a peek.

How much did you write? How many words? How many sentences? What did you write about? Did the time pass quickly or slowly? Were you surprised about what you wrote? Did you learn something? How did you feel? I hope you stopped after five minutes. Your goal in this chapter was to experience the act of writing, for no particular reason other than to see if writing in this way might appeal to you. Who doesn't have time to write for five minutes everyday? As you continue to read this book, you will have many other opportunities to write. So designate one of your least precious notebooks to be your writing companion. If you do, you will have the best chance of realizing the point of writing and appreciating that you are the one who cares.

Beliefs to Consider Making Your Own

1. Writing is a process that needs to be experienced.

Experiencing the writing process before you think you are ready is essential. Don't wait until you have finished reading this book! While this book will offer you helpful advice about how to get started writing, it will not reveal any big secrets about writing or offer a foolproof method. All writers agree that you just have to sit down and begin. Writing needs to become a habit. You need to experience the satisfaction of putting down one sentence after another and filling up a page with your thoughts. You need to experience the feeling of discovering a thought you weren't aware you had, and you need to realize that you have ideas.

2. Free writing is the easiest way to get your ideas down on paper.

Simply putting your pen or pencil on your paper and writing your thoughts is a good way to get started writing. Anything and everything is acceptable. Even if you find yourself writing *I have nothing to say* over and over again, keep going because you may have a censor sitting on your shoulder. Know that this is a possibility especially if you have high expectations for yourself and you're more product oriented. But keep at it. You have nothing to lose and eventually your brain will engage with your pen and thoughts will emerge.

3. Lower your expectations.

Freeing yourself from the idea that it is possible to produce a polished, finished product each time you sit down to write is an important goal to keep in mind. Even your favorite authors can't do it, despite all the books they have written. Remember that their books are the finished products of their painstaking efforts. Lowering your expectations will allow you to experience what it feels like to simply write. The benefits you feel as a result of free writing will be more relaxing and satisfying to you than a finished product will ever be, because you are learning about the *process* of writing.

4. Establishing a new habit takes time.

Think about the last time you decided to embrace a new habit. It may have been a commitment to exercise, to eat breakfast every day, to eat more fruits and vegetables, or to save more money. Establishing the writing habit will also take time, but the advantage of writing is that you will immediately have concrete proof of your effort each time you date a page in your notebook and just write!

CHAPTER TWO

What Are You Worried About?

Get it down. Take chances. It may be bad, but it's the only way you can do anything really good.
—**William Faulkner**

The act of putting our pen to paper brings up all sorts of anxieties that get in the way of writing, even if we remember that we are just writing for ourselves. Unfortunately, our worries are not going to go away. Confronting and understanding them is vital so that they will not divert us from realizing our goal.

Worrying begins the first time we sit down to write. Instead of congratulating ourselves for taking the first step, we hear a little voice inside us saying—*What do you think you're doing?* This is the first of many voices we will hear as we grow into our writing habit. Some of us may even feel self-conscious writing in our own homes, unless we are fortunate to have a separate office space. Even then, we worry that if our spouse or child should knock on the door and ask what we are doing, we can hardly imagine saying to them, *Oh, I'm just writing.* The thought that they might question us even further about *what* we're writing or *why* we're writing is terrifying. What would we say? Because we've just begun, we can't possibly offer a satisfactory answer either to ourselves or to anyone else. We can, however, use the question as a directed free write. Here's one of mine that I wrote at a local coffee shop.

> To be honest I have no idea what I'm doing and I hope that no one sees me sitting at this corner table with my cup of coffee. My pen is moving along a random line in this scruffy little notebook, which I figured was good enough. Even though it looks like the pages might fall out I like the fact that the pages are small because maybe I'll actually fill up a page and maybe another. But why? I still don't know. Is this really writing? What's the definition of writing? Putting down one word after the other? Wouldn't it be funny if someone happens to look in my direction and imagines that I'm really a writer? What is a writer? Someone who writes? After all I <u>am</u> writing even though no one except me can see what I've written. I don't think anyone is really looking at me or really cares what I'm doing. I really am writing for myself and for some reason it feels good. Next time, I might even answer one of my other questions.

At first, our task is to just sit down and write *something*. We need to experience what it feels like to write. As we begin to realize that we are able to string one word after another, we see that we can fill up a page in our notebook with our sentences, with our thoughts. This helps us to broaden our definition of what it means to be a writer. If we transport ourselves to a public place where we can maintain our anonymity, we may feel safer trying out our impersonation as a writer.

By confronting this very fundamental worry, we will eventually be able to answer that little voice that haunts us. We realize that writing is a task that we can physically do because we possess the rudimentary skill that's involved in simply getting words down on paper. We just have to make ourselves do it. It doesn't require expensive equipment and we don't even have to enroll in a class. In the privacy of our own notebook we see our words grow into sentences. Our thoughts materialize. We read and reread them. As long as our expectation is not one of a polished finished product, we can accept this very basic definition of what writing is. We are not writing stories or poems or letters. At this stage, we are not even writing to communicate with others. Our writing is for our eyes only and all we require of ourselves is to be a kind and patient audience.

Is this kind of writing enough for us to sustain a writing habit, though? For a while it might be, but only if we are able to address another worry that is a universal problem, and that is the issue of time. We never feel that we have enough time to accomplish all the things we *have* to do in our lives, not to mention the things we'd *like* to do. We try to master the art of multi-tasking and realize this comes with an increasing level of stress. We experiment with a myriad of organizational strategies and electronic devices with no better result. As counterintuitive as it may sound, writing is exactly the kind of pursuit that provides us with at least a short-term solution when we make it a priority. It gives us time for ourselves. It slows us down. It relieves stress, as I discovered in this free write.

> Today I was actually looking forward to writing! How can this be? Even though I had tons of other things to do this morning, I knew I had to write. So I did. I know that it might not be for very long but it will be time that I can spend with myself with no other agenda than to sit down and collect my thoughts. It feels like fun. Never before have I associated writing with having fun but there I've said it. Starting to write without a plan or specific purpose feels so freeing—so relaxing. I wonder where the words come from one right after the other with no inhibitions. At some point they stop but then I get to reread what I've been thinking. Unlike talking when my words disappear, written words allow me to inspect them—to see what I'm thinking. It's definitely me-time.

When we sit down to write for ourselves, we experience what it means to use writing as a tool for thinking. If we are working at a job that requires a solution to a problem, we can use writing as a tool to help us address it. If we are struggling with a family issue, writing helps us think through ways to understand and manage the situation. If we are plagued by a personal concern, we can use writing to explore our feelings. Once we realize the practical application writing has to our everyday lives, we are more likely to look forward to spending time alone with our pen and notebook. The pages we fill provide tangible evidence of how we've spent our time. Writing has a built-in accountability feature.

Using writing as a tool for thinking, however, may lead us to another worry. What if we uncover something in our writing that is troubling? This is a distinct possibility in the uninhibited flow of free writing. The discovery aspect of the writing process can motivate us to return to our writing again and again, but uncovering a worrisome situation can be problematic. What do we do about it? This certainly happens to me every now and then as this entry reveals.

> If I'm honest with myself, which I'm going to try to be this morning, I realize that I often won't let my pen take me wherever it wants to go. I know I'm fearful of writing about my younger sister's tragic and tumultuous life that ended at the age of 57. I've never written very much about my father perhaps because of so many regrets I have about our relationship that had so many unresolved issues. And then there's my mom who's still with me nine years after her death. I've certainly written about her but also censor my efforts more times than I would like to admit. If I were more of a "real writer" I'd consider these darker sides of my life the raw material for a good short story or even a novel. But somehow, going there as the kind of writer I am feels like I'm using writing as therapy. Perhaps I'm not yet ready to get involved in a therapeutic relationship with myself. Am I afraid of where my writing will take me? Am I afraid of who might read my words someday?

This is a kind of writing we do not share freely with others. But often our darker thoughts reveal universal themes that are compelling ideas. Censoring our writing is something we consciously or unconsciously do, understandably, because it reveals an important truth about writing. When we write we think. Writing on a regular basis helps us to lead our lives as thinkers. We attend more deliberately to the events in which we are involved and ideas that concern us. We are curious about people we meet and wonder about their stories. We are more observant of our surroundings. We are mindful of our environment and we try to make sense of our world.

Going down this path is a good sign for it means that we have more raw material and ideas for writing than we once believed. What begins as a worry is actually a potential opportunity for us to write about what matters. Coming to this realization takes time, but once this occurs we're on the way to developing a writing habit that is sustainable. Every day of our lives we have thoughts and ideas that are potentially worthwhile. In fact, we have more than we once believed possible.

When we sit down to write, we now have confidence that we will come up with ideas to write about. But this good news leads directly to yet another worry. Are our ideas good enough? What's our definition of a good idea? How do we determine which of our ideas are good ones? We wonder—*Good for what? Good for whom?* If we believe that we're truly writing for ourselves and we are our first and most important audience, then perhaps our criteria for what is good should be the extent of our interest and investment in the idea. If so, this interest may lead to more substantive pieces of writing.

It's happened again. I knew what I was going to write about before I picked up my pen this evening. I seem to be obsessed about the number of monstrous mansions that are invading our neighborhood. As I walked up the block this evening I spotted a

FOR SALE sign on the little yellow Cape sandwiched between a newly erected "hotel" as some of our neighbors have described it and the "castle" on the other side. It's been vacant for a year so I predicted it would probably be the next victim. Unfortunately I was right. What draws me to this topic? Am I just venting or is there something more to this idea? Is it inevitable that this will be another teardown? Why do I keep coming back to this idea?

This one actually did lead to a poem called "Helpless" that you'll see in chapter ten. As we periodically reread our entries, with a highlighter in hand, we search for patterns in terms of the topics about which we have written. We may notice the raw material for a letter to a friend we haven't seen in awhile. We see several entries concerning an issue in the news we feel passionately about. This might be a sign that a letter to the editor of the local newspaper is percolating inside us. We notice a few lovely phrases and images about observations we've made with the changing of seasons and wonder if we could craft a poem to capture our impressions. We find bits and pieces of a humorous experience we shared with our child and think about composing an anecdote to preserve the memory. But to do this, our words need to be well written.

The key to believing that we have good ideas is linked to the very legitimate worry about the quality of our expression. Our censor is constantly with us and hard at work, prematurely evaluating and judging our written expression before we have engaged in the revising and editing process. Free writing, when practiced often enough, will promote writing fluency but often results in run-on sentences, lack of punctuation, and spelling errors. Our confidence can be easily undermined even as we become more fluent writers.

> Why did I ever decide to reread some of my writing? Who am I kidding? I can't write. While I still get a kick out of some of my ideas, this morning all I could see were the run on sentences and spelling mistakes. I notice that when my sentences are really long I have to reread them in order to figure out what I'm trying to say. Sometimes there really is something there and other times I'm just confused. Why can't I seem to think clearly all the time? What a ridiculous question that is. Thinking is hard work and seeing the evidence of my thinking in writing I guess proves that very fact. How can I not get discouraged though?

We realize that the free writing we generate for ourselves is an exploration of what we are thinking. We are writing quickly. We are not revising our thoughts or editing our sentences. But revising and editing are also part of the writing process and there is no reason to believe that the process occurs along a straight linear path. Once we have ideas that we believe are good ones because they keep drawing us in, we naturally want to tinker with them so that they become clearer and crisper. Our curiosity about what we are thinking may motivate us to revise and edit solely to clarify our ideas for ourselves, but this leads to another worry.

> It's been a few months now since I have somehow found the time to sit down and write. My free writing has allowed me to generate a fair number of entries in this notebook. I have even

solved a few work related problems when I've posed questions to myself that I need to think about. That's been good—a very practical reason for writing but what do I do with the rest of this stuff? Occasionally I'll reread it. Some of it is worth rereading for the memories it brings back but then I wonder. Am I just wasting my time? What's the point?

If we feel that writing is a waste of time, then we're definitely not going to pursue it. Perhaps the easy part, now that we've accomplished it, is getting started. How are we going to sustain our writing habit? We experience this feeling when embarking on any new habit or activity. If we decide to practice piano, then we know we have to commit ourselves to practicing day after day or we won't progress. If we need to do stretching exercises to increase our flexibility, then once a week isn't going to be enough. Writing offers us more flexibility because what we hope to get out of it will affect how much time we devote to it. After we have found a reasonable entry point, which is what free writing is all about, we may find ourselves at a plateau if we want to seriously create more polished pieces of writing. However, if we are deriving pleasure from free writing with no need to go any further, then we'll be content with our musings. I have felt both ways as illustrated in this entry.

The thought has occurred to me that I might just want to do something with some of my writing. As I flip through my notebook it's clear that I've got a lot on my mind. I've done a good job solving some problems at work. That's been very utilitarian writing. I've preserved some memorable experiences I've had with my family through words, which almost feels like what a photograph captures. Some of my writing is just venting and when I reread it I realize that it too served a useful purpose. Do I throw that kind of writing away or do I keep it as a reminder?

What worries do you have at this point in your writing journey and how will you address them? Absolutely nothing is riding on whatever efforts we make at writing. We have the luxury of writing for the sheer pleasure that it brings us. We can write as much or as little as we desire. We don't have to revise and edit our words. We don't have to show anyone else what we've written. We are not faced with deadlines or expected word counts. We are in total control of what we write, when we write, and why we write. In time it may even become a pleasurable pastime.

Confront Your Worries

I. How would you answer the worries discussed in this chapter?

How will I explain to myself why I am writing?

How will I justify the time I need to write?

What if I discover troubling thoughts?

How will I know when I uncover a good idea?

How will I deal with my censor?

Do I have a need to "do something" with my writing?

2. Use writing as a tool to address your own worries.

What are your questions? Make a list. Which one will you answer first?

3. Take time periodically to reread what you've written.

Never underestimate the value of periodically rereading what you've written. With a kind heart and a highlighter in hand, force yourself to take note of a random word or phrase that adequately captures a thought or an idea. Note topics that you frequently address and wonder why. Use your reflections to inspire more writing. Know that you are at the beginning stages of collecting ideas for future writing.

4. Consider revising and editing some of your entries to clarify meaning.

The writing process is not a linear one. It is perfectly fine to revise and edit any of your free writes or directed free writes to clarify your intended meaning.

Even though you are writing for yourself, rapid writing is often confusing. Revisiting and revising your favorite entries enables you to experience the satisfaction of working out what you are trying to say.

CHAPTER THREE

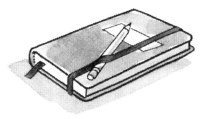

How Will a Word Photo Help You to Get Started?

What one does is what counts.
Not what one has the intention of doing.
—Pablo Picasso

I am not inclined to make New Year's resolutions for it's been my experience that I never manage to keep them. However, one that I made several years ago was different. It had to do with my interest in making time to write on a regular basis despite an increasingly busy life. I must admit that the idea wasn't completely original because my friend Edie inadvertently prompted it when she told me about her resolution.

Edie had decided on New Year's Eve to take one photograph a day during the upcoming year. It was an ambitious undertaking, but she loved photography and wanted to be a better photographer. She hoped that the task of finding a photo every day would recapture the excitement she had felt five years earlier when she attended a week-long photography camp in Maine. When I met her in mid-January at our writing group meeting, she reported that she had taken two weeks worth of photos having committed herself to never leaving home without her camera. I listened, happy for her resolve, knowing that I could never imagine engaging in such an ambitious task. Still I was curious about how she was going to decide what to photograph each day and so I asked her.

"My days at school are packed with constant interactions with kids so I'm sure they will be the subject of some of my photos," Edie began. "Then there are times when something catches my eye when I least expect it. It could be a reflection in a window or someone crossing the street. You just have a hunch that might be a good shot so you snap it." I understood what she meant. She then continued, "Even seemingly mundane events, upon future examination, offer insights into who you are and how you make sense of your world. I know I'll also take photos of friends when we get together, or Ray's softball team, or even my yoga class." Edie then pointed to the fireplace with one hand as she held her camera with the other. She winked at us before admitting, "I knew you'd all be my photo for today. Sometimes, I have to admit, I know ahead of time." As we began our meeting, I couldn't help but want to continue the conversation. "So what do you see as a connection between photography and writing?" I asked.

"I guess the closest connection," Edie replied, "is being able to capture those small moments we all refer to in writing. I do know that with my camera in my hand I'm a better observer of those small moments. I'm not convinced that I'll write anything about my photographs, at least not the majority of them, but you can never tell." Edie then proceeded to show us the photographs she had already taken. The range of subjects that she had captured on film captivated us. While some experiences had personal meaning for her alone, others had universal appeal and became the springboard for much discussion.

In the days to come, I found myself continuing to think about the offhand comment Edie had made about the possible connection between photography and writing. One day, I thought of the book *Journey* by Patricia MacLachlan. It was a children's book that I had saved from my teaching days. Unlike many others, this one had found a place on my shelf next to my favorite books about writing. Was it because of the way photography had figured prominently in the story of an eleven-year-old boy who searched photographs for answers as to why his mother had recently abandoned him? Was it because his grandfather, with whom he now lived, was constantly taking photographs for no apparent reason? The grandfather explained that perhaps people take pictures "to see what is there." My scribbled marginal note indicated that I was intrigued by the idea. The photos the grandfather took were seemingly random shots, but each had an undeniable emotional quality that transcended the scene photographed. Each said something. Photography was indeed an outlet for discovery and self-expression. While some photographs are significant only for the photographer, others may resonate with a broader audience. I thought about writing and believed it served a similar purpose.

Shortly after our writing group meeting, I made my own New Year's resolution. Instead of using a camera, in the manner that was second nature to Edie, I decided to use my notebook and pen. In mid-January, when my New Year's resolutions usually begin to fade, I committed myself to a rather quirky way of maintaining a journal. Each day I would *pretend* to snap a picture of a person, place, or object that for some reason had captured my attention. It did not have to be a special occasion or an unusual experience. It was rather about finding something interesting in whatever I happened to notice or wherever I happened to be. Unlike taking a real photo, I simply jotted down a brief caption in a chunky spiral-bound notebook that I vowed to have with me all the time. Later in the day, I would write a few sentences about my "snapshot." I became a better observer of my surroundings and my feelings as the following two entries show.

January 15 **"Apple Tree Outside My Kitchen Window"** — I just love looking out my kitchen window each morning while I'm having breakfast. I often feel a guilty pull between reading the newspaper or just staring out the window and noticing what's happening outside. Today the tree branches that are delicately covered with snow are winning and why not? Winter has just begun and the tree looks so beautiful as does the yard with a light blanket of snow covering the perennials. I wonder how they're doing under all that snow.

January 16 **"Gail Ann's Donut Shop"** — I think about how long I've been coming here to write on Saturday mornings. After my errands are done and I've been to the gym, Gail Ann's always beckons. Today, in addition to my journal, I have this "Word Photos" notebook. Do the owners ever notice me sitting at the corner table lost in my notebook with my pen in hand? Probably not. That's what makes this place such a comfortable spot to write.

While two consecutive entries did not guarantee a regular writing routine, I considered it a good omen that I had at least started. During the next two weeks, I took "photos" of a variety of people, places, and objects. I was amused by what captured my attention and surprised by the words that came off my pen. Was there really a connection for me between quilting and writing as the following entry suggested?

> **January 25 "Beautiful Print Fabric"** — Every time I begin a quilting project I have the same self-conscious thought. I take perfectly good material, cut it up into squares, triangles, and rectangles and then proceed to reassemble them to make a pleasing pattern which turns into something useful or something pleasing to look at. I had a vague plan for this table runner at the outset but then I see so many other possibilities. Quilting is a little like writing. It's creating something from nothing! Is this why I like to do it? So many of my hobbies have this quality. Stitch by stitch I knit a sock. Note by note I play a melody. Line by line I draw a picture. It's a process of discovery and revision.

As Edie had suggested a connection between photography and writing, I discovered an unexpected connection between quilting and writing. It reminded me of a favorite anecdote in Anne Lamott's book *Bird by Bird,* which was also on my bookshelf not far from *Journey.* As the story goes, Anne's brother was immobilized by the huge task of trying to get a report on birds written. Apparently the deadline was fast approaching and her brother was overwhelmed. Her father sat down beside him, put his arm around his shoulder and said, "Bird by bird, buddy. Just take it bird by bird." How often am I reminded of this wise advice when I'm engaged in an overwhelming task? In this case my overwhelming task was establishing a new writing habit. Writing one page at a time, one day at a time would be the way to start.

At the beginning of February, I decided to date the next twenty-eight pages of my notebook to see me through the shortest month of the year—another good omen. I then went one step further to solidify my commitment. I grabbed a black sharpie marker and boldly titled my violet covered notebook "PHOTOS That Have Never Been Taken." Its manageable size seemed perfect for the amount of time I decided to devote to the task. My plan was to write a new entry on just one side of the page. If I didn't skip any pages, I would have enough room for three hundred sixty-five days. I remember flipping through the pages and visualizing what the notebook would look like if I managed to fill it, taking it "bird by bird." I wondered what I would write about. Would it be fun for me to reread my words or would it be a boring recap of insignificant events?

During the next month, I took "photos" of a variety of people, places, and things. I never knew at the start of the day what I would be attracted to, although some days, as Edie had said, I had a hunch. While I sometimes obsessed over what would be the perfect photo for the day, I soon talked myself out of this notion. I didn't want to complicate matters. If I wrote down a caption early in the morning and then a better or more significant scene captured my attention in the afternoon, would I be disappointed? Would it be better to wait until the end of the day to make my decision? But, what if I forgot? Ultimately, I decided it didn't matter. I would just make the decision at some point during the day and stick with it. After all, if this idea had any merit, there would be a next day and a next day. I was right.

When I embarked on this project five years ago, I had no idea that year would also be the year that my younger sister, Ellie, would die at the age of fifty-seven, after a long battle with breast cancer. Indeed, I never imagined that four months after her funeral I would be diagnosed with an early stage of the same disease and would undergo two surgeries and six weeks of radiation. Not surprisingly, forty-nine of my entries that year focused on my sister. Even though she passed away in February, she was connected to many of the snapshots I took throughout the year. The following are examples of my remembrances.

March 27 "Bead Department at Playtime" — As I started over to the cash register to pay for my skein of yarn, I glanced over to the bead department and immediately thought of Ellie. Just last summer we were here together. We had so much fun looking at all the beautiful beads and I remember how hard it was for her to make a decision. She kept asking me for my opinion. Little did I know that she was planning to make a necklace for me and wanted to be sure I'd like it. A tear rolled down my cheek as I realized we would never again be able to shop for beads or for anything else. I still wear the necklace.

November 9 "Corridor at Lahey Clinic" — I sit alone in the corridor, waiting my turn for the set up for the final eight sessions of treatment. The radiologists refer to it as the "boost," which is a bit unsettling. I think of Ellie. I realize how impossible it was for me to fully appreciate all she must have been going through when she underwent more than just radiation. I remember her talking about the anxiety of various procedures and then waiting for test results. I thought I understood. Now I understand better.

Two other themes characterized my entries that year. Twenty-nine were about my son who was then a graduate student and another forty-four I broadly characterized as having to do with nature. As had been the case with my sister, I took the "snapshots" of my son at times when he wasn't even present! The ones about nature often occurred while I was driving to work in the morning or returning home at the end of a long day. These, too, prompted other surprising free associations that revealed to me what was subconsciously on my mind.

August 26 "Red Line at Harvard Square" — The little boy bounded into the car and announced to everyone that this was his first subway ride. His grandmother smiled as she adjusted his stroller and took a seat next to him. She then reached into her tote bag and took out a zip lock bag of pretzels and gave it to her grandson. I had a flashback to Ted and how much he loved subway rides...pretzels too. I regretted having to get off at the next stop.

February 2 "**Dashboard Digital Clock at 5:00**" — I'm longing for spring and have been regularly checking out the sunrise and sunset times that are posted in *The Globe*. Tonight, while driving home, I was excited when I noticed that it was still moderately light at 5 pm. Spring is coming even thought the groundhog saw his shadow today.

While there were predictable annual events that I felt compelled to capture in a word photo, the remaining entries that first year were one-of-a-kind occurrences. As I flipped through the pages, reading whatever caught my eye, I still began to notice some patterns. I became intrigued by the prospect of trying to understand what I chose to write about and, more importantly, why. What mattered to me? What might I discover about myself? I thought about Edie and her photography. Hadn't she said something similar? When I looked more carefully at the word photos about places, for example, many involved tables—friends gathered around a table eating. I was struck by how many were around tables either at my own home or at the homes of friends, and not necessarily at holiday times. Others were at restaurants, but not necessarily related to a special occasion. They were small but important moments.

July 3 "**Betsy and Drew's Porch**" — This porch is one of my favorite spots to be on a summer night. It's like a tree house overlooking their untamed and overgrown backyard. We gather around their small round table artfully arranged with appetizers and drinks. We talk and tell stories. We laugh and reminisce. We have dinner. Betsy lights candles and serves dessert. We are best friends with a long history since our college days and our kids are like cousins.

October 14 "Jakes in Northampton" — If I lived in Northampton Jakes would be my favorite place to have breakfast. I could tell everything was healthy and wholesome the minute I walked in the door and the atmosphere was so friendly. The waitress said it all when she greeted us with "Is your morning off to a good start?" When we said, "Yes," she said, "Well, it's about to get even better!" She was right, and all we had was scrambled eggs, home fries, and toast.

Suffice it to say that every time I reread my word photos, I was struck by how many memories came rushing back to me. How was it possible that this happened time and time again and with so few words? Although I certainly wished that my word photos could have been more skillfully and expressively written, I was happy that at least they were there. I decided that the quality of my writing was adequate for the purpose the word photos served.

I reminded myself that my goal was to establish a daily writing habit and to give myself the opportunity to discover the range of topics that could be the basis for further writing. Still, I was pleasantly surprised when I occasionally discovered a few more expressive entries like the following two.

April 29 "Orange Pansies" — I look down at my perfectly ripe and sweet mango. It's so easy to scoop out the sweetness from its own little dish. As I do, I look out the window and suddenly notice the pot of pansies I recently bought. I was attracted to this particular one over the more typical purple and yellow ones and wonder if it might have been named Mango.

August 18 "Sparrows in the Birdbath" — Who was their leader I wonder? It was as if some little sparrow said the town pool for birds was having a grand opening in the Hannigan's backyard. There must have been more than a dozen sparrows that accepted the invitation to go for a dip. Flitting back and forth from the top of the fence to their pool they seemed to be taking turns diving in and splashing about. I tried to take a real photo with my camera but it didn't do the scene justice. Neither do these words but I tried.

Word photos have continued to be an enjoyable way for me to pay attention to my life, in the moment, as well as to reflect upon those moments at future times. When I was working, especially the year before my retirement, I was struck by how often I snapped a photo at work. I had resisted doing this at the start of my project because I wanted to reserve the idea for the times when I wasn't working. I was striving to lead a balanced life and believed that writing would help me. However, work was also a part of my life. The snapshots I took at work, especially during that year, were valuable for a number of reasons. Later, upon rereading many word photos, I realized what a wonderful experience I had had as an elementary school principal. I also discovered why my decision to retire when I did made sense, as the following entry showed.

April 5 "Full Moon Driving Home at 9 pm" — I love my job BUT it's the night meetings that get to me. As I look up at the moon and realize how long I've been away from home today, the only positive thought I have is that tomorrow we have a day off. I've begun to count down the number of monthly evening meetings that I'll need to attend for the rest of this year. I'm glad I've made my decision to retire.

When I started my first "PHOTOS That Have Never Been Taken" notebook, it was not much more than a New Year's resolution. Because I did enjoy writing, I thought it would be an easy and very accessible way to maintain a habit despite my increasingly busy life. I knew that writing had a calming effect on me and helped me achieve a balance between work and home. I knew that I was enamored of the discovery aspect of writing. I never failed to learn something as a result of my writing and I loved the fact that often my musings were amusing.

I eventually realized an unexpected benefit to this kind of writing. At the end of the year, when all the newspapers and magazines ran stories about the major events of the world, I decided to embark on the task of trying to figure out what constituted some of the major events in my own life. As I arbitrarily flipped through the pages, I became intrigued by the prospect of being able to categorize them in some way. I was curious what they revealed about my place in the world.

One summer day, I made myself a tall glass of lemonade and headed out to the Adirondack chair in my backyard. I had my chunky notebook in one hand and a simple computer generated chart in the other. The left hand portion of the chart had a place for me to record the date and photo caption for each of my entries. On the right hand side, I listed the following categories: people, places, events, objects, nature, and work. I began by examining just one month. I reread each of the entries and assigned them a category. Sometimes there was an overlap but when this happened I made the best decision I could. I kept reminding myself that this was an assignment I had given to myself. I could continue or abandon it at will. As it turned out, I worked through three months that first day. During the next few rainy summer days, I completed the remainder.

As you might well imagine, when I embarked on this task I was glad that I was in the privacy of my backyard. In the same way that I had felt self-conscious about snapping a word photo with my pen, I felt even more self-conscious categorizing my entries. Although a bit compulsive, I convinced myself that one could say that about any researcher, and research was what I was actually doing. With that thought in mind, I carried on with a task that proved to be gratifying for me in many ways.

First of all, categorizing my entries satisfied my curiosity. Writing for me is all about thinking. I was interested in what these little snippets of thought revealed about what was on my mind. As a workingwoman as well as a wife and a mother there were always competing demands and never enough time to simply slow down and think. Writing, for me, became a way to do just that.

The second benefit had to do with my desire to achieve a healthy balance in my life. Being mindful of the need to slow down and really pay attention to people, places, and events at home and at work was one way to achieve this. Although I hadn't deliberately planned that "nature" would be one of my categories, I was pleased when I discovered that I often took the time to note seasonal changes.

Finally, I realized that my notebooks provided the raw material for future writing projects if and when I had the desire. I didn't necessarily need to search for books of writing prompts and ideas. I didn't need to wait for a special occasion or a vacation to have something to write about. Small, seemingly insignificant events held meaning for me. I believed my pen helped me to make connections and to discover what I was thinking and why. I never knew exactly where my snapshot would take me and I loved that.

June 18 "Young Woman Walking Six Dogs" — Every time I see this woman walking six dogs I have to laugh. The dogs look quite happy and must consider themselves part of a special club. Two stately golden retrievers, a dignified black lab, two fuzzy yappy ones, and a Brittany Spaniel mix that brings back memories of Spody. It's been almost thirty years since she died and I still carry her nametag on my key ring. Today it was like seeing her again.

November 18 "Bob's Eyes" — As soon as I got home from work and Bob greeted me I could tell something was wrong. I could tell it in his eyes. When he said I have some bad news to tell you so you'd better sit down, I did. I knew it was about Paul. Paul's cancer has metastasized and the prognosis is not hopeful. I thought we would all be growing old with Paul.

Getting started on the road to writing begins with putting your pen to paper on a regular basis. It's about observing bits and pieces of your everyday life and the odds and ends that make it what it is. It's about paying attention and gaining confidence that you indeed have ideas. It's about lowering your expectations and being kind to yourself. It's about establishing a new habit. Your reward will be a sense of satisfaction and calm from writing again and again in this manner. Snapping a "word photo" is a strategy to help you get started. It's about not expecting a polished, finished product each and every time you sit down to write.

Creating Your Own Word Photos Notebook

1. Get the right size notebook that will set yourself up for success.

Consider trying out a chunky spiral 3½ x 5½ notebook. They come in a variety of bright colors and are easily available in most drug stores. With two hundred ruled pages, you'll have sufficient room for a year's worth of "photos" if you write on both sides. Composing three to five sentences a day, generally fewer than one hundred words, is a realistic goal for even the busiest individual. You of course may need to lower your expectations if you tend to be a perfectionist, but remember you are the only one who will be reading your words. If you pick too large a notebook, you'll feel compelled to fill up the page and it will take more time than you may want to devote to the task. It's best to start small.

2. Date the pages one month in advance.

Dating the pages is not only a way to commit yourself to the idea, but it will also prevent you from ripping out pages if you don't like what you've written. This kind of writing is not intended to be a finished product. You are recapping your stream of consciousness thoughts. Another reason to date the pages is that you won't be able to change your mind about the photo you've selected. You're trying to train yourself to just "go with the flow." Don't make a big deal out of your selection. You're simply trying to establish the habit of writing. What you write doesn't have to be clever or creative. You do not need to revise, edit, or censor your efforts.

3. Decide where you're going to keep the notebook.

Being able to locate your notebook is important because you never know when an idea is going to capture your attention. When I was working, I always had my notebook in the car. When I retired, I kept it on my desk at home. It could also be in a backpack, a purse, or a briefcase. If you've got another idea, give it a try.

4. Begin each entry with a caption.

The caption should be whatever words will capture the essence of your idea. Even if you don't have the time at that very moment to write your thoughts about your snapshot, the caption will serve as a useful reminder.

5. Let your sentences flow.

You might start out simply stating what you observed. The second sentence will extend your thought a bit further and the third sentence still further. Write as if you're talking to yourself. You are your audience. You might wonder why you selected this image. You might pose a question to yourself about your observation. Try to let the thoughts in your head flow into your pen and onto the page.

6. Reread what you've written.

Rereading what you've written is a good habit. You want to be sure you haven't left out any words, which can sometimes happen when you're writing quickly. Sometimes your handwriting can be unclear, so rereading ensures that you'll be able to decipher your words on another day.

7. Congratulate yourself.

Give yourself a pat on the back each time you complete a page in your notebook. You're on the road to creating memories of small moments that will remind you of people, places, objects, and events that you experience in your day-to-day life.

CHAPTER FOUR

How Do You Start Thinking Like a Writer?

One of the things that happens when you give yourself permission
to start writing is that you start thinking like a writer.
You start seeing everything as material.
—Anne Lamott

If you've been pushing yourself to engage in free writing and you've started snapping more word photos with your pen, then you're well on your way to thinking like a writer. Yes, I said *writer*. I can't think of any other word to describe someone who writes. While we consider writing a hobby rather than a career, we can still benefit from some of the practices to which many professionals subscribe. Maintaining a writer's notebook is one such example. In this chapter, we will explore what a writer's notebook is, why you might be ready to experiment with the idea, and how it can be another way to make writing a pleasurable pastime. It will also inspire you to start thinking like a writer and paying attention to your life.

I first became aware of the idea of a writer's notebook over thirty years ago, while attending a summer writing institute at a local college. During the course of the weeklong institute, I observed one of the presenters surreptitiously pulling out a small brown notebook from his shirt pocket every now and then. Sometimes it was while one of his colleagues lectured. On other occasions it was when a student spoke. At other times it was during lunch when he appeared to take a break from our conversation, in which I innocently thought we were all engaged. I was not alone in observing his behavior. As the week drew to a close, I finally mustered up enough courage to inquire about his practice.

"Hey, Manny," I tentatively inquired. "All week I've been noticing that notebook of yours that you keep pulling out of your pocket. What do you write in it?"

"Oh, that—you noticed," he sheepishly smiled. "I'm sorry…it drives my wife crazy, but I'm afraid it's a habit."

How could he possibly have thought that no one would notice? Some of us even thought he was rather rude. As he continued to talk, we realized that he really couldn't break himself of a habit that served him well.

"It's kind of hard to explain to you exactly what I write or why, because I'm not even sure I know. And besides, you would probably think that some of what I write is rather silly. Maybe it is." He paused for a moment and then continued. "But what I can tell you is that most of the articles and stories and poems and even books I have written all got their start in one of my notebooks." That was a significant revelation.

Even though Manny was not willing to show us or even to read some examples of what he wrote in his notebook, he gave us a couple of suggestions. He said that he often jotted down an intriguing thought he had while driving or walking. He liked to capture bits of overheard conversation when he was at a diner or on the subway. It was fun for him to note the playful language on a bumper sticker or a billboard. His notebook was his way of helping himself pay attention to his environment and to what was happening around him. While I didn't remember too much else about the course, I do believe that my current practice of carrying a small spiral-topped 3 x 5 notebook started shortly after that course ended.

Many authors, who have written about effective writing instruction, include information about writer's notebooks. Lucy Calkins and Shelley Harwayne, in their book *Living Between the Lines,* promote this practice when working with elementary and middle school students. I have been inspired by Ralph Fletcher's practical and generous suggestions in *Breathing In, Breathing Out: Keeping a Writer's Notebook.* I have appreciated the wisdom of Georgia Heard's lessons in *Writing Toward Home.* What was most valuable to me was the process of trying to figure out how to maintain a writer's notebook that would work for me. As is true with so many things in life, doing is key to understanding.

Before I even knew what I was going to write in my notebook, I was obsessed with trying to figure out what kind of notebook would be the right one for me. It took me five years of trying different kinds before I settled on the one that has now become my trademark. My first three were quite small—3 x 4. I remember how happy I was to find them, four to a package in an assortment of appealing colors with no side spiral to interfere with my left hand scrawl. But by the time I had reached the midpoint in the first one, the pages had started to come out. This cute notebook with the gummy binding was not strong enough to secure its eighty pages for more than a few weeks. Even though I still had three left, I searched for another type.

My next purchase was about the same size although it had many more pages. I only bought one, having learned from past experience and because I wasn't convinced the spiral on the left hand side was going to work for me. However I wrote in it quite a bit. I loved that it fit in all my pockets and with its bright yellow cover it was easy to find in my purse. But when I needed another one, I couldn't find a replacement. In desperation I made another selection.

This one had a side spiral, which my left hand was getting used to, but a bit larger in size. I remember debating long and hard about the size and thickness, but I thought it would be worth a try since I sometimes felt cramped by the smaller one. With its two hundred pages though, it simply lasted too long! The front cover eventually came off, some of the beginning pages ripped out and, for the last few months, I held it together with staples and an elastic band.

When I needed a new one, I found yet another style that seemed vaguely reminiscent of the one Manny used several summers ago. Despite the fact that it was the ugliest notebook I had ever seen, it had three potentially important features—it would fit in my pocket, it had machine-stitched pages, and no uncomfortable spiral. But the proof is in the using and somehow I didn't use it very much. Within weeks I replaced it with another 3 x 5, sixty-page standard "memo book" with a colorful cover that I knew I could always find in any drugstore or supermarket. Like magic, it was the right fit for me especially because it had a spiral at the top! Eventually I bought them in packages of five at an office supply store.

As you begin to experiment with the idea of a writer's notebook, finding one that seems right for you is important. Only you will know based on your preferences and idiosyncrasies. Of course getting the notebook is the easy part. Figuring out what to write in it is the challenge.

My first notebooks were filled with what Manny had characterized as word play in the environment—clever uses of language, funny expressions, bits of overheard conversations, and amusing things people said. Suddenly I found myself tuning in to language in a way that I never had before. When I spotted clever words and phrases on bumper stickers, signs, restrooms, and t-shirts, I made it a practice to jot them down in my notebook. When I heard playful words coming out of the mouths of the children with whom I was working, I did the same. Indeed when I had a child of my own, I discovered that he too would inspire me with an endless trove of humorous expressions and insightful observations. Finding time to jot them down without being conspicuous or rude was often a challenge. Some inspired word study lessons with students; others found their way into poems I was writing; and others simply reminded me of a good time and made me laugh. Here are some examples:

On a sign outside a museum: Please do not tread, hop, step, trample, plod, tiptoe, traipse, meander, creep, prance, amble, jog, trudge, stomp, or walk on the plants.

Overheard observations of children:
My tooth is like a tire swing that goes around and around.
You put a pyramid at the end of a sentence.
Did you know that every name begins with a letter of the alphabet?

On restroom doors:
Buoys and Gulls (a seafood restaurant)
Menhatten and Queens (a NY style delicatessen)

In addition to word play, I also found myself writing quotes that I found interesting in whatever I happened to be reading—from professional books and journals in my field as an educator to novels, magazines, and newspapers. Not surprisingly, many of them were related to the writing process, while others had to do with my work as a teacher of writing. I don't know if Manny did this, but it really didn't matter to me because it gave me an opportunity to use my notebook. To this day the words of others continue to inspire me and my writer's notebook gives me a place to store them. In fact many of the quotes that begin each of the chapters in this book came from some of my earliest notebooks.

Although I suspected that Manny's entries were more "writerly" than those that ended up in mine, I reminded myself that he was an author and I was not—at least not yet. For this reason I tried not to become discouraged when I found shopping lists and to-do lists among some of my entries. I was still trying out the idea and this too may happen to you.

Are you wondering at this point about the connection between free writing, snapping a word photo, and beginning to maintain a writer's notebook? If the distinction is starting to blur in your mind, then the practice of free writing has afforded you the opportunity to write without censoring your efforts. Snapping a word photo has inspired you to become an astute observer of your environment. Your writer's notebook will be the place to consolidate your efforts as it becomes a collection of free writes, word photos, jottings, and bullet points. They will not be finished pieces of writing, but rather kernels of ideas. Some ideas might materialize into longer and more coherent pieces, while others will remain undeveloped.

Frequently I would pick up an old notebook at random and reread it from cover to cover. Other times I would flip through it searching for something I vaguely remembered having written. I likened the experience to cleaning out a closet or going through a dresser drawer. I never knew what I'd find or what would catch my fancy. Often it was fun to simply recall a moment with no need to do anything more with it. On the other hand, sometimes I'd find an idea that made me think I had more to say. Free writing has taught me, as I hope it has taught you, that the act of writing helps you to discover what you're thinking. You are your first audience. Once you've experienced the fun of writing for yourself, you will find it enjoyable to sit down with the idea of giving that gift of words to yourself.

So what do entries in a writer's notebook look like in addition to examples of word play and inspirational quotes? When I was a teacher, some of my earliest entries were ideas that would help me craft a piece of writing that I would share with my students before giving them an assignment. When we were working on character sketches, for example, I found the following notes based on a situation I had observed while riding the bus.

> On the bus:
> Such a hot, steamy day
> Noticed a young man sitting across from me
> Bright pink tank top, HUGE black Reeboks
> Oversized gym bag between his hairy legs partially obstructing the aisle
> Desperately trying to open a small package of peanuts—I could relate to that!
> Coke can balanced on his gym bag
> Intent concentration
> Innocent looking
> Used flip top from can to open the bag—finally!
> Blood on finger

Two months later, I used my notes to write a first draft of a character sketch that I then shared with my students to help them with their own writing. As a teacher, my notebook was coming in handy.

Snack Time

A huge, husky young man dressed in an oversized pink tank top and loose fitting black shorts sat across from me on the bus. Squeezed between his size twelve running shoes, a duffel bag bulged at the seams. On top of the bag, balanced between his hairy tanned legs was an opened can of Coke Classic. In his hands he struggled to open a bag of peanuts, which would complete his afternoon snack. First, he lifted one end of the bag to his mouth, to bite off a corner, but the cellophane seam held tight. He then tried shoving the peanuts up and over to one side of the package but to no avail. Finally he shook the bag of nuts and when they hit the top of the can he smiled. In no time at all, he worked the flip top lid loose and used it to slice open the bag. Success! I smiled at him as I got up from seat to get off at my stop. It was then that I noticed the trickle of blood coming from his finger.

As writing in my notebook became more of a habit, there were many other such examples. In the following one, I even included a bit of overheard dialogue that I worked into the short anecdote I called "The Spirit of the Season."

Shopping at a favorite gift shop:
"I've been looking all over for that color lavender."
"Would you like it?" Took it off over her head.
"You can try it on if you'd like." Held it up to her
"I know it will fit you just fine. I got it at the church exchange.
"When you're finished, pass it on. I'm hot anyway."

What's the point?
About the owner and the friendly quality of the store?
About being swept up in the holiday spirit of giving?
About the customer?
About literally giving the shirt off your back?
About the reaction of the other customers?

The Spirit of the Season

A few days before Christmas I was trying to finish up my shopping at one of my favorite gift stores. Standing behind the cash register at the small counter was the owner of the store who was engaging in the kind of friendly chitchat that is her trademark.

"What a lovely sweater," she told a customer, the first in a line of many customers who were patiently waiting their turn. "I've been looking for one in that shade of lavender for years."

Out of the corner of my eye, I noticed a woman's arms stretching to the ceiling as she proceeded to remove the garment that had just won her this compliment.

"I'd love for you to have this sweater," the woman said. "I bought it at our church exchange and I've had it several years. Please try it on."

Taken aback, her face slightly flushed, the owner quickly assured her that it would fit and tried to continue with the sale. The customer persisted.

"Really, I'm hot and I want you to have it. When you're finished, you can pass it on."

"Well, thank you," the owner stammered. She quickly folded the sweater and tucked it under the counter. And so the woman left, leaving us all to speculate about what had just happened. I wondered whether the owner would ever compliment a customer on her attire again.

Although I embarked on my habit of keeping a writer's notebook when I was a teacher, I must admit that once it became a habit, I found that I could trace a great many of my more polished pieces of writing straight back to my 3 x 5 notebooks. While writing personal narratives was a useful link to my classroom teaching, I also found that genre to be a way to preserve family memories as well. Over the years, on numerous occasions, I recorded an event in my notebook that I would later craft into an anecdote or a poem. Each completed piece preserved a memory with more detail and emotion than was true of a photograph alone. Every now and then I would even share a piece with an appropriate family member or friend as a gift of words.

I found letters to be a very useful form of writing. Some letters were of a personal nature while others were letters to authors whose books I had enjoyed. I regret that I don't do this often enough because I've heard that authors enjoy getting mail from their readers. Sometimes I've mustered up enough courage to write a letter to the editor of a newspaper to voice my opinion about an article that may have touched a raw nerve. Although I was successful in having just one actually appear in print, I don't for a moment regret having written the others. In every case my writer's notebook became the place where I could play with my thoughts and ideas in order to clarify my thinking. Since I have been keeping a writer's notebook, I have also written several articles that have been published in teaching magazines and journals, and even two books! Manny was right.

While recounting the number of entries that became more significant pieces of writing, I also had a hunch that a number of potentially valuable ones were lost within my growing hodgepodge collection of notebooks. At that point, I decided to number and date my notebooks on the front covers with a bold black marker. I was now able to respond to my friends who often asked how many notebooks I had, but this new practice did not make it any easier to find what I was looking for as my collection continued to grow. I currently have well over one hundred and also a manageable indexing system that enables me to find what I'm looking for with relative ease. While you might not be prepared to do this at this time, the idea is worth filing away for future use. If I had started the process right at the beginning, I would have saved a great deal of time, but who knew?

My index system is in a loose-leaf notebook organized in the following six sections: word play/dialogue, ideas for anecdotes/poems, notes for letters/meetings, reflections from conferences/classes, quotes, and bibliography. As I complete each notebook, I take the time to reread each page and force myself to make a snap decision about which category would be an apt classification for the entire entry. I then jot down a very brief summary of the entry with just enough information to remind me of its potential for a longer piece of writing. It requires a quick reading, not getting lost in the memory, synthesizing the entry in a short phrase or two, and then jotting down that brief synthesis on the designated sheet of loose-leaf paper. Sometimes if the entry is long I just note "look back" or "promising" to remind me that I may want to revisit it. Sometimes it is, and sometimes it isn't, but the strategy works for me.

Not surprisingly, the "idea section" was really the heart of my writer's notebook. As I periodically reviewed my index, I noticed that at times I had optimistically made notes, but upon further examination, very few entries appealed to me. However, every now and then I would run across a notebook that I considered to be rich in potential ideas. For example, in "Book 94" I found ideas for two poems that captured my attention. One called "Twilight Zone" was the first to emerge. A few months later, "My Poems" came into focus. Unlike the previous examples, the following entries were single words or phrases that occurred to me at unexpected moments during the time I was participating in a weekly poetry group.

Book 94 (excerpts)
Digging in the soil—favorite spot to think—splendor of fertile ground
While the censor sleeps, the inspector is off-duty—Twilight Zone?
Unencumbered—unfettered—agile
To play with words in the uninhibited grandeur of a middle of the night dream? reverie?
Another poem? first line?
Most poems start out in the shallow end—dog paddle about with childish enthusiasm
How do I describe my poetry group friends?
Surer strokes? Words of Wisdom? Deeper Depths (alliteration)
My teacher—gentle nudge, well placed push
Ending to my poem? Approximations close enough to stand up to the day light zone

Twilight Zone

To play with words
in a middle-of-the-night
reverie
is to know the splendor
of fertile ground.

While the censor sleeps and
the inspector is off-duty,
words drift and flow
in an uninhibited swirl
unencumbered
unfettered
agile
as they audition.

In night-time's
mind's-eye view
all words are worthy
contenders
stand-ins
understudies.

Hope abounds
as they brave
the scrutiny
of the daylight zone
when perhaps
a couple might just
get the part.

My Poems

that start out
in the shallow end
dog paddle about
with childish enthusiasm
at last so glad
to be moving about
staying afloat.

But they long to do better.

They go in search of
other paddlers
who have surer strokes,
and words of wisdom.
Real swimmers
who will spur them on
to deeper depths
with a gentle nudge
or a well placed push.

Not all notebook entries hold equal potential, but many do. I prove this to myself when I periodically make the time to reread my index with a highlighter in my hand. As I come across an entry that has been the raw material for something more significant, I highlight it. It's a game I play and I continue to be astounded at the number of entries that have led to longer pieces. This indicates to me that an idea takes a long time to incubate until it's ready to emerge.

In short, the writer's notebook is yet another tool to help you to consolidate the efforts you've made so far in the process of thinking like a writer. If you like the idea, you may even start numbering your notebooks. That might be an indication that an indexing system of some sort is in your future as well— another good sign. You will then have your own personal stockpile of potential ideas to write about because you've been paying attention to your life.

Starting a Writer's Notebook

1. You need to decide on a notebook that is a practical choice for you.

Getting one that is small enough to fit into your pocket makes sense, because you can be sure that you'll always have it with you. You never know when an idea is going to find you. A small one is also easy to conceal so you won't feel self-conscious about carrying it around with you. On the other hand, if your handwriting is large, a small one might feel too constricting. Give it some thought, make a decision, and live with it for a few weeks. If it's not right, you'll know and can then make a better choice.

2. Select a notebook that has a good binding.

Spiral bindings or those with stitched pages are the best because the pages don't fall out. If you're a leftie, a spiral at the top may be a good option, but again it's a personal choice. A trip to a local stationery shop or office supply store will offer many options.

3. It can't be too fancy or too thick.

You want a notebook that you don't mind messing up. If it looks too precious, you might have a tendency to censor your efforts. Remember you're just collecting ideas. The problem with getting one that is too thick means that it's going to last a long time. When you're just experimenting with the idea, starting with a smaller number of pages is better so you can have the satisfaction of filling it right to the very end. You'll then be excited about beginning a brand new one.

4. You'll most likely have to remind yourself what the purpose of your writer's notebook will be.

Make a list of the following ideas to get you started—overheard conversations, word play, word photos, questions to ponder, interesting words, favorite expressions, details, phrases, quotes, etc. Don't be dismayed if on occasion you find a random grocery list, recipe, or reminder. Just turn the page and go on.

5. Be sure to make time every now and then to reread what you've written.

If you do, you'll be amazed at all the observations and thoughts you have. Your words will bring back memories. Over time, you may notice patterns in terms of your interests and feelings. Some of your entries will inspire you to write even more. Maybe you'll write an anecdote or a poem or a letter or maybe even a book some day!

Chapter Five

How Can a Journal Be More Than a Journal?

*Writing is not a process of recording details
but of making significance of them.*
—**Lucy McCormick Calkins**

Many professional authors sing the praises of journaling as a means to gather ideas and reflect on experiences. Others claim that too much journaling is really a procrastination device, which prevents them from making progress on a book, article, poem, or story. For our purposes, though, which is after all to make writing a more significant part of our lives, the idea is worth investigating. In this chapter we'll explore a few reasonable ways to maintain a journal. We'll consider the benefits of each approach in order for you to decide which one appeals to you. There's no right or perfect way to keep a journal. The best way is the way that will work for you.

I came upon the idea of keeping a journal in my twenties. My first journal was a lovely batik-covered blank book that lasted five years, which gives you an idea of how regularly I wrote in it. Still, journaling was the beginning of a process I went through, as I was curious about the role writing could play in my life. After having taught for six years, I was suddenly unemployed, having moved to another part of the country for my husband's job. Many of my entries, especially at the start, were short, very mundane, and quite inconsequential. But I'm willing to share a small number with you, since we've been together for the last four chapters.

June 9 — I'm feeling a bit apprehensive about not having gotten another job lined up yet. At least I've had some interviews and I think I've done fairly well. It seems like such a political system dependent on whom you know and I know no one! At least not yet.

June 20 — The Red Sox lost after 14 long, boring innings and I broke a tooth while watching the game. I really didn't need to have popcorn, which is what aggravates me. At least I have a good dentist to go to even if he does terrify me.

June 24 — It's been great having Mom visit but today when she left she said she was going to Long Island to visit her cousin, not back to Florida. Tonight Dad called and wondered when Mom was coming home. I didn't know what to tell him. He sounded very worried that she wasn't coming back. Could it be that she's leaving him? It's not the first time she's thought about it but I'm glad she didn't consult me. I'll bet she's talking to Jennie.

July 11 — I haven't gotten much sleep lately. There have been many, many calls to and from San Francisco. Ellie has finally decided she's had enough. After a tumultuous three-year marriage she's leaving Randy. She's spending the summer with us. My job search is going to come to a screeching halt!

In time my entries did improve in quality as well as in length. Some, in fact, I am very pleased to have. They bring back significant memories during a period of time that included an extended job search in a large urban area and a career change from classroom teaching to staff development. I was also called upon to help my sister who was in an abusive relationship from which she literally needed to escape. That summer my mother had decided to separate from my father, much to his chagrin. The last few entries documented the trauma of our beloved dog's battle with cancer and her early death. Two years into this first journal, I made what for me was a startling revelation.

> **November 14** — It's been much too long since I last sat down with this book and how I regret not having the discipline to write on a regular basis. It seems that I'm often motivated when things aren't going well or I'm out of a job or I'm in the midst of sorting out a perceived crisis. Today I've had a really good day…the first one in two weeks following aggravation upon aggravation at work and the extraction of two wisdom teeth. I need to remember this day and force myself to write in order to reflect on important aspects of my life, both at work and on the home front. I need to try to make the time. I want writing to become a habit.

When my son was born, I immediately knew what to do with a beautiful journal that a friend of mine had given to me. I had considered its marbleized cover, in shades of green and gold, too pristine to mar with my scribbles. When Ted was born, I was glad that I had saved it for a special occasion.

I maintained that journal fairly conscientiously during the first few years of his life. I didn't write in it every day, but I did write often enough to capture memories that I will always treasure. During the first fifteen months, when I was fortunate enough to be a stay-at-home Mom, I began to establish the habit of writing. When I went back to work, I wrote more sporadically but still I was determined to keep up the pattern I had established.

This journal really convinced me of the pleasure of writing just for myself. I used writing to document the details I felt were important to remember as I was learning how to be a mother. Early on, I jotted down observations about Ted's eating habits and sleeping routines. I noted changes in his behavior and issues I wondered and worried about. Glancing back at earlier entries helped me gain perspective on how we were doing as a family. I often consulted my journal when we were going through a rocky patch to see what insights I might glean from past experiences.

When Ted began daycare, I continued to write but not with the same regularity. The first entry, which didn't occur until November, revealed my anxiety about how I was going to continue to write as I was now back to a full time job in addition to being a parent.

November 28 — Day care has been a huge success but I haven't written a thing about what's been happening there. I'm trying to figure out how to organize my thoughts to sum up what's really important since I last wrote...How about this... August remembrances...September remembrances...October remembrances...and now it's November! YIKES.

I decided that not all of my entries needed to be in complete sentences. Phrases were fine and occasionally that's all that I had time to record. As Ted's language developed, I loved to jot down some of his expressions. I was happy that I had noted his changing preferences in terms of his favorite toys, foods, books, clothes, songs, and stuffed animals. How I wish I had recorded even more than I did. You think you're going to remember, but you don't.

When Ted entered kindergarten, my journaling took a different form. One day prior to the start of his first day of school, I grabbed whatever notebook I had on hand and I wrote the following letter to him.

Dear Ted,

This week you'll be going to kindergarten and although I'm sure you're ready I'm not sure I am. It's been a rough time for me. I've treasured these last five years with you. I love the times we color together, take walks, go out for lunch, and just fool around. I learn from you to pay more attention, to slow down, to play, to pretend, to enjoy the present. While I don't want to be one of those moms who has to have a blow-by-blow description of everything that you've done all day in school, I still hope you'll share just a little about what you're doing with me.

Love,
Mom

During the course of my son's kindergarten year, I filled three 5 x 8 notebooks with letters to Ted. I found myself squeezing in time to write whenever I could during those first few weeks of school. Later, as routines were established, my entries developed a predictable rhythm although hardly a predictable pattern in terms of their content. Sometimes I wrote a page, sometimes two or three, depending upon where my pen took me and how much time I had. I considered it to be a new way to keep a journal. It was a place for me to record my reactions to my child's entry into the world of school. As a teacher myself, I needed to develop confidence in the way in which another teacher was going to educate my child. I needed to make the transition from a very comfortable and cozy daycare center to what at first seemed to be a huge and impersonal public school.

At the same time as I began writing my letters to Ted, his teacher initiated a more public correspondence that, much to my delight, came home every Friday in my son's backpack. Her weekly messages were dedicated to "all the families and friends who ask their kindergarteners, 'What happened at school today?' and get 'Nothing' for a reply!" I was fascinated by the way she summarized the week's activities in a way that served a number of purposes. Her words not only gave me confidence that Ted was indeed in good hands, but she also educated me about what the kindergarten year was all about from her perspective. One evening in October, when I returned from Curriculum Night, I wrote the following letter to his teacher instead of writing to Ted!

Dear Ms. Yardley,

I don't even know how to begin to convey my appreciation for the thoughtful, purposeful, and caring classroom environment that you described this evening at Curriculum Night. Everything you said made so much sense. No wonder Ted loves school. I admire you and am so thankful for your being Ted's first introduction to what learning could and should be like in a public school.

Ted's Mom

I must confess I was a bit self-conscious about this new practice of mine. Although it took me very little time to realize that Ted's introduction to public school was going to be everything I had hoped for him, the transition was a more challenging time for me than it seemed to be for my son. After all, Ted had Ms. Yardley to help him; I was on my own. What I did have was my pen and notebook, which helped me work through the ups and downs of *my* kindergarten year as a parent. When I looked back over the very focused journal I kept during Ted's first year in school, I was struck by how emotionally laden the process of parenting a child through school is. Writing in my journal truly helped me through the process.

The next opportunity I had to maintain a *focused* journal occurred seven years later when I turned fifty. At that point in my educational career, I became an elementary school principal— a role that at one time would not have had the slightest appeal to me. And yet, I couldn't pass up the opportunity even though I was not entirely convinced I would be able to meet the challenge. I knew, however, that I had a pattern of turning to writing to help me reflect on new situations.

During the first three years of my principalship, I held to a weekly pledge to converse with myself on paper. I wrote at a local coffee shop on most Saturday mornings for as much time as it took to drink a ten-ounce cup of coffee. When the coffee was gone, I was done. Setting a time limit was a useful strategy because the routine did not become a burden. Best of all, at the end of my writing, I was ready to carry on with my work with renewed optimism and confidence. Writing afforded me a much-needed opportunity to slow down and think. Inspecting the somewhat random thoughts that came off my pen was illuminating. My goal was not to record everything that happened, but rather to make sense of the issues that came tumbling across the page. I was looking for significance in the details as the following excerpts reveal:

September 16 — I find that I'm trying to be the kind of principal that I would have liked to work with when I was a teacher. I think I'm also subconsciously thinking about trying to emulate some of the positive qualities of principals I've worked with in the past as I also steer away from the negative qualities I remember—how not to be. Just as a parent hopes their child will embody the best qualities of each parent, I hope to take the best from everyone who has influenced me as I create my own identity...

April 27 — This week I realize how much I love this job. I also realize how much it is a process of growing into it, seeing my role more clearly and the great potential it has for shaping a school in certain ways. I certainly am beginning where people are—both staff and parents. I haven't come in with a preconceived notion of how things "should" be but just some basic tenets and the desire to engage everyone in the process of growing our school together...

October 25 — I'm struck by how a school can actually muddle along haphazardly. That's how so many of the schools I've worked in have functioned. I realize how much I don't want this to happen at my school. I want this school to run smoothly. I want everyone to feel invested. I want this school to make sense.

My official principal journal ended at the end of my third year. I took this as a sign that I didn't have as urgent a need to use writing as a tool to help me grow into my role as a new principal. I was well on my way to running a school that made sense and my writing was focused in other genres—essays, articles, stories, and poems. Still, I often used my 3 x 5 writer's notebook to work through problems and issues I needed to think about, but no longer did I have one place to keep all my musings. It just didn't seem necessary anymore and so I stopped.

The focused journals I've described were an excellent bridge to the "commonplace book" journals that have now become my preferred format for journaling. I write in them on a very regular basis. I even make time to reread them periodically. I was inspired to try out this idea after reading an article by Beverly Beckham in *The Boston Globe* called "When Your Memory is Merely Jogging in Place."

As I am crediting Beverly Beckham for the idea, she actually credited her daughter's high school teacher. According to the article, her daughter "came home from high school with a blue exam book and a glue stick. Her assignment was to cut and paste and write or scribble anything that she felt like pasting or scribbling, to use this booklet as a kind of scrapbook, not just of her thoughts but of her life." As she watched her daughter happily fulfilling her assignment, she decided to join her. Shortly after I read the article, I did as well.

The first item I pasted into my journal was a beautiful black and white photo of my mother when she was a child. I could only guess her age because like most old photos we find, at least in my family, it was not dated. I couldn't ask my mother, because she had just passed away a few months before, and I was struggling to live my life without her. My second entry was Beverly Beckham's article, underlined with selected passages that would guide and inspire me. My third entry was my commitment to embark on this new way of maintaining a journal.

> **February 14** — Finally on this snowy Valentine's Day, I begin the process of trying my hand at keeping a commonplace book journal inspired by Beverly Beckham's article that caught my eye November 6, 2006, a couple of weeks before Mom died. It was one of those articles I saved and I'm glad I did. I think this journal might be a kind of "healing" journal reflective of the things I've been doing since Mom died...I'm ready to plunge in, willy-nilly. Like quilting, there doesn't have to be one way to do it. It's the process and, like my writer's notebook, I will learn by doing. Unlike other journals I've kept in the past, this one will also

include a variety of common items—photos, articles, mementos, souvenirs, and who knows what else. Of course I'll write in it as well. It may have the feel of a kind of illustrated scrapbook.

My prediction was absolutely correct. My first commonplace book provided me with a place to *focus* my thoughts and attention on how my life was going to be during the first year without my mom. Initially I believed the journal would become a very focused collection of writing about my mother and that's certainly how it began. But in addition to my written entries, I often included the words of others—poems, articles, essays that I had run across in the past and had placed in a box for safekeeping. Others were newly found pieces that seemed to find me at just the right time.

I also placed photos and other souvenirs in my journal that reminded me of my mother. I finally had a place to put the various "artifacts" that I had saved in the past for some reason. I'll bet you have some of your own stashed away in the bottom drawer of your desk or in a box in the back of your closet behind your shoes. Each of them brought back a significant memory that prompted a journal entry.

The only problem I encountered was that the journal was a more cumbersome book to deal with, unlike one of my trusty 3 x 5 notebooks, which I always had safely tucked away in my pocket or purse. In order to write in my healing journal, I had to plan ahead. I noticed that the time I often spent with my journal was a Saturday afternoon, which was the time I would have been talking with my mom on the phone. Perhaps it was not surprising then, that a little more than two months into this experiment, my entries took the form of letters—letters that couldn't be delivered but served a similar purpose as our weekly long distance phone conversations. I was convinced that writing would once again help me to work through what I was thinking and feeling. Writing a letter to my mother helped me to catch up with myself.

As I neared the end of this journal, I wondered whether there would be another. The idea of having a focus might have been functional for me at the time and fulfilled an important purpose. Would I think of another compelling reason to begin another book? Had I thought to do a quick Google search of commonplace books, I would have found many inspirational ideas, not to mention numerous sources to explore. I may also have embarked on many detours and distractions that would have prevented me from simply opening up another blank book and beginning, which is exactly what I did.

I picked up another journal and started writing. I decided that this would be my second commonplace book and it, too, would have a theme as suggested in the first entry.

January 14 — Today, not surprisingly a snow day, I have decided I will use this book in the weeks and months ahead to help me know when will be the right time for me to retire. I look upon today as a "free day"—one that I have the luxury of doing exactly what I want to do. That's how a snow day always feels to me and I can't help but wonder if that's how retirement will feel. Will I have more energy to do the things that are so hard to make time to do while I'm working? Or will too much unscheduled time make me less productive? I wonder.

Completing this journal took a little over two years. I was intent on thinking about retirement and how I would know when the time was right for me to make the big decision. The written entries were candid and served as excellent documentation of what I was thinking. The various artifacts I collected included ticket stubs from concerts, museums, and baseball games—things I enjoyed doing in my free time. I listed books that I was reading and my reactions to them. I included poems that I loved and I copied quotes that held meaning for me. Some essays and articles were about retirement. When my contradictory feelings finally sorted themselves out, I made the decision to retire and set a date that was two years away.

Since then, my commonplace journals have not been theme oriented. Rather they are simply about my life and I am so glad to have them. I've come to believe that my commonplace book is a gift to myself.

May 23 — I like the idea of beginning my new commonplace journal as I begin my 61st year. This one will not have a specific focus but will just be about my life—a life rich with friends, good health, a happy marriage, a son who will graduate from college tomorrow, and a job that I love—most days. In two years, I'll probably retire.

When I make the time to reread these journals, they reveal a snapshot of my life—the joys, sorrows, challenges, dilemmas, experiences, and important events in a calendar year, give or take a few months. They reveal the unexpected occurrences, experiences, and complexities of my life and my attempts to reflect on them. Some sections are certainly topical—my bout with cancer four months after losing my sister to the same disease, for example—but they are juxtaposed with other entries that show how life goes on.

As aging tends to bring thoughts of downsizing, the consolidation of my life onto the pages of a book that I can review at will is appealing. My journal helps me to reflect on how I'm living my days and holds me accountable to paying attention and to valuing what's important. My only regret is that I didn't start sooner.

Considerations for Journaling

1. Are you ready to explore journaling as a way to make writing a part of your life?

As you've probably gathered from this chapter, there is no one right way to maintain a journal. While I am currently a fan of the commonplace book, I've had the opportunity to try out other approaches and each has its advantages. If you have started a journal in the past and then abandoned the idea, consider why this happened. If you want to sustain the habit of journaling, do it in a manner that brings you satisfaction.

2. What kind of approach makes sense to you?

The focused journals are more likely to have a clear purpose from the outset and eventually, once their purpose is realized, they come to a logical end. The emphasis can be of a personal nature or work related. While the commonplace book is less purposefully focused from the outset, it won't preclude a focus, if that's where your pen takes you. The commonplace book could be an advantage for you, if you like the idea of incorporating artifacts along with your words, or a turn-off, if you can't imagine enjoying its scrapbook-like quality.

3. What kind of notebook will suit your needs?

Journals have become an increasingly appealing item to buy in a variety of stores, from drugstores to bookshops to office supply stores. While a simple spiral notebook may be exactly what you need to get started, you may also be drawn to a more handsome bound book filled with lined or unlined pages. If you like to draw, unlined pages are especially useful. A spiral bound book may more easily accommodate the artifacts characteristic of a commonplace book, but not necessarily. I have used both kinds with equal success. Thickness is another consideration as well as size. You have to get one that is just right for you.

4. How often, how long, and where will you write?

By this time, after having experimented with free writing or word photos or entries in a writer's notebook, you know the importance of setting yourself up for success. What's manageable for you given the other pressing responsibilities in your life? Is once a week realistic? Does once or twice a month sound better? How about a day of the week that you could easily see yourself building into a routine? And where will you write? Is it difficult for you to find an uninterrupted period of time at home? Would you do better to treat yourself to a cup of coffee or tea and write for as long as your drink lasts? These are decisions that only you can make.

CHAPTER SIX

How Can You Start Reading Like a Writer?

Reread what you've written. Listen to what it's telling you.
What does it want to be? A poem? A story? A memoir? An essay?
—Georgia Heard

As you've gathered by now, this is not a book filled with prompts and ideas about what to write. Rather the book is designed to inspire you to gain confidence in your ability to think like a writer, which means coming up with your own ideas. The word photos you've captured, the free writing you've done, your reflective journal entries and accompanying artifacts, provide ample evidence that you've got a feel for what it means to think like a writer. Now it's time to start reading like a writer.

This chapter explores some ways in which the words of others can provide inspiration for transforming the raw material you have been gathering in your various notebooks into more polished prose. To accomplish this you'll need to be on the lookout for short, well-written pieces found in the magazines and newspapers that you enjoy reading. Unlike novels and non-fiction books that are also useful models for effective writing, shorter forms like personal essays, letters, poems, op-ed pieces, anecdotes, and articles are more accessible for our purposes. In addition, because they are based on personal stories, they enable us to see how we too can draw from our own experiences.

The words of others can also provide inspiration for our own writing in terms of their format and style. Have you ever read an anecdote in a magazine about a comical situation with a child that brings a smile to your face? As you're perusing the newspaper, perhaps an essay on a topic that you've been thinking about appeals to you. You nod your head in agreement, and suddenly realize you're engaged in a silent conversation with a person you may never meet except though their words. You may even feel that the essay was written just for you! Or, maybe you're struck by a poem. You find yourself quietly staring into the distance moved by the poet's words. You might read it a second or a third time and wonder how a few well-chosen words can elicit such a powerful reaction deep within yourself.

The number of writers I've vicariously met through the essays and columns they have written astounds me. In fact I have a loose-leaf binder that houses a collection of writings that I have gathered over the years. It's a random assortment of articles from the mundane to the serious reflecting subjects of interest to me—childhood, dogs, aging, holidays, humor, teaching, technology, time, parenting, and of course writing. I clip them out and place them in my notebook because they resonate with me. Some capture an idea that I want to remember. Others I may want to share with friends. Indeed I often do rummage through my notebook to reread a piece that I vaguely remembered having tucked away. I suppose my collection of writings illustrates how much I value the words of others.

Over the years I've gotten to know columnists in my local newspaper, *The Boston Globe*. Beverly Beckham, Bella English, Ellen Goodman, Donald Murray, and Linda Weltner are just a few of my favorites. They write about topics that seem to find me at just the right moment in my life. While they write about experiences based on their own lives, they are not self-indulgent. Rather they make a connection with me and engage me in reflecting upon a similar experience in my own life. They transcend the personal to express a universal message. While Donald Murray is no longer alive and others have retired, I'm fortunate to still have their words.

Now is the time to start your own collection of writings that resonate with you. Stash them in a box or folder or notebook for safekeeping. They will inspire you to begin the process of more conscientiously reading like a writer. What appeals to you? Does the opening sentence draw you in immediately? Are the details so specific and vivid that you find yourself forming pictures in your mind as you're reading? Are the sentences so clearly written that you have no difficulty following the writer's message? Do you ever wonder if this polished piece might have started out as a word photo or a succession of free writes? This last question is perhaps the most important one to consider.

Since you've been experiencing the writing process for yourself, you now realize that a well-crafted piece takes time to compose for novice writers as well as for professionals. Published copies are painstakingly revised and edited. Indeed, you will be able to transform some of your initial ideas into a polished piece with steadfast effort and resolve. This is where your collection of inspirational examples will come in handy.

A useful place to begin is to examine the lead sentence of some your favorite writings because getting started is always a challenge. How do authors do it? Some begin with a startling fact or a question. Others may choose to begin with an action statement. Still others start with a description of a character or a place.

Stating a fact, asking a question, showing action, and describing a character or location are just a few possible types of leads. As you begin to read like a writer, focus your attention on the opening sentence. Does it draw you in? What kind of lead is it? Make a collection of your favorite leads. When the time comes for you to transform an entry from your writer's notebook into something more, you'll have a couple of models to guide you. As you're beginning to amass your own collection though, feel free to incorporate any of the following lead sentences taken from various anecdotes and essays I have written. Which ones would invite you to keep reading and why?

Each April first the roses appear—sometimes red, sometimes yellow and last year, the most beautiful shade of coral. ("April Fool's Day 1984")

"I hear something," Ted said as he jumped up on the couch and pulled back the curtains. ("Ted's New Bed")

With her broad smile and sparkling eyes, Maria made eye contact with each of her customers as she sashayed from table to table. ("Ranch-o-Casados")

Freddie is not getting the attention to which he has become accustomed and so he storms back to his desk swearing that he will not write today. ("Freddie")

While each of these leads ultimately resulted in a completed draft, I found that brainstorming several before beginning to write in earnest helped me to discover the most potentially promising direction. You may find the same is true for you.

We can say the same about titles. Do writers think of a title first or does the title come after writers complete their drafts? My experience is that the title comes after I've discovered what I'm writing about, but I often come up with a *working title* to help me focus initially. Very rarely am I wedded to it. As the lead sentence is a hook to get you to read an entire piece, the title will invite you to begin. When I look at just the titles of the articles in my loose-leaf notebook, I always gain some insight that can help me.

Some titles are simply declarative sentences that give the reader a hint about content. Other authors tend to craft minimalist titles that are effective in arousing our curiosity, but may not give as clear a hint as to what will follow. Some are a play on words or have an alliterative quality, while others are subject to a variety of interpretations.

Again, I offer a few titles from my own writing that illustrate these techniques.

"Not the Way It Was Supposed to Be" (about purchasing a wedding ring)

"The Rotation" (about using a baseball metaphor to describe my son's weekly dinner requests)

"The Cafeteria as a Classroom" (about making a school cafeteria a civilized environment)

"What a Way to Be" (about an intergenerational friendship)

You're probably asking yourself at this point—But how do I make my writing worth reading from start to finish? As you're going through your collection of articles and essays that have captured your attention, first by the title and then by the lead, you then need to pay attention to words, phrases, or sentences that made you stop and reread. Maybe you stopped because the author painted a vivid picture. Authors refer to this as "showing rather than simply telling." The following examples taken from two different anecdotes illustrate this idea.

Ellie jumped up spilling her glass of orange juice on one of the many Lake George brochures that was lying on the kitchen table. This summer was the first time we were not going to visit relatives. Instead we were going to a place that Ellie thought might have been named after our Dad. I didn't think so but for all I knew she may have been right. ("First Vacation")

"Why would you want to make one of those?" my mom asked as we stood in front of the assortment of model airplanes at Grants 5 & 10 at the University Plaza where Mom always did her shopping. My reward for having to tag along with her on a Saturday morning was not only a slice of bologna from the butcher shop but also a trip to Grants. Grants was filled with all the diversions a ten-year-old like me needed to spend a happy summer day on our screened-in back porch. ("A Gift for Dad")

Another useful strategy is the use of authentic dialogue that brings the characters to life and helps you get acquainted with them. This example is from "What a Way to Be," mentioned earlier.

"My name is Jan," she said with a twinkle in her eye as she gazed around the table at the gathered group of aspiring poets, "and I've always wanted to write a poem. I decided at my age— I'm 93 by the way—it was about time that I tried." She never mentioned that she was a prolific author of young adult and children's books and had even written two books of humorous and poignant essays about being old when she was in her eighties.
When she called me a couple of days later to ask for a ride to class, I was happy to help her out since I lived close by. "Now before you say yes so fast," Jan said, "you need to know that I don't

move very quickly, my hands don't always do what I want them to do, and on top of that I come with a walker."

"That doesn't bother me," I said. "I'm retired; I'm not in a rush anymore. We'll just leave enough time."

Having a strong emotional reaction to the words of another person whom you don't even know makes you think that the writer is talking directly to you. I hope this thought will motivate you to capture moments in your life that you feel are important enough to preserve for yourself. A good way to begin is to answer the question posed by Georgia Heard at the start of this chapter: "Reread what you've written. Listen to what it's telling you. What does it want to be? A poem? A story? A memoir? An essay?" All forms require attention to engaging titles, effective leads, relevant detail, authentic dialogue, and careful attention to word choice. Some of your free writes, journal entries, and word photos can be revised to produce a short yet satisfying written product.

As you begin to do something more with your raw material, you may very well uncover a topic or subject that wants to become something longer—perhaps an anecdote or an essay. Not surprisingly, being able to compose a longer piece from start to finish will take some time and patience. Your first attempt may be a very long and rambling one. This is perfectly natural as you're in the process of trying to figure out what you're attempting to say. In fact, a long and cumbersome sentence is an indication that you're working out an idea. This is also true of a rambling paragraph. Some words may be repetitive. Perhaps a sentence is unnecessary. A very useful strategy to try, if you find yourself confused about what you're attempting to say, is to impose a word limit on yourself. Try one hundred words to start. Increase the number to two hundred fifty. Set a cap of seven hundred fifty. A word limit forces you to make every sentence count in the same way that writing a poem requires a very deliberate and intentional choice of words. You are forced to clarify what you're thinking. So now is the time to start laying the foundation of "doing something" with your writing.

This will be easier once you start to build your own collection of writings that will inspire you. Think of them as mentor texts. Be on the lookout for short examples that resonate with you. Figure out why you like them. If you find one on a topic that appeals to you, then feel free to try your own hand at writing something similar. The topic is probably worth exploring, but your version will not be exactly the same as the one you just read. Experiment with several leads before settling on one. Think of a good working title to maintain your focus, but be on the lookout for a better title that is embedded somewhere in your developing draft. Consider where you can incorporate some dialogue to move your tale along. Practice *showing* not just telling. Have fun discovering what you mean to say and write on!

Tips for Reading Like a Writer

1. Put your writer's notebook to new use.

As you're reading the newspaper or articles and stories in your favorite magazines, have your notebook by your side. Be attentive to the pieces of writing that draw you in and try to figure out why they do. Could it be the catchy title? Could it be an engaging lead sentence? How would you classify the title or the lead? Does it exemplify any of the samples discussed or have you discovered a new one. Jot it down so you'll remember it.

2. Pay attention to what you're reading.

Do you have some favorite columnists in the newspapers you regularly read? How about the magazine section of your Sunday paper? What kind of human interest stories appeal to you? Do you like anecdotes? Are you drawn to op-ed pieces or letters to the editor? What topics or ideas do you care about?

3. Start making a collection of writings that appeal to you.

Cut them out or copy them. Find a place for them in a manila folder or envelope or loose-leaf binder. Do you see any pattern to your collection? Are you attracted to essays more than anecdotes? What about letters and poems?

4. Take time to reread your own writing.

If you've been successful in making writing a habit, you have a great deal of raw material that can be transformed into a more polished piece of writing. What does your writing want to be? What you like to read is often a clue as to what you're going to enjoy writing, so give it a try. Don't be afraid to set a word limit for yourself.

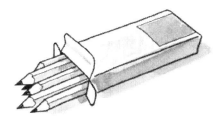

CHAPTER SEVEN

Why Not Start a Writing Group?

As I reach out to create the writing communities I need,
I have one rule; I do not share my writing in process with anyone
who does not make me want to write.
—Donald Murray

Twenty years ago I, the novice writer that I perceived myself to be, actually started a writing group! Even more amazing is the fact that it exists today. In fact many of the original members still attend our monthly meetings. I now believe, with considerably more conviction than I had at the start, that participating in a writing group is a good idea. I also believe that starting one of your own, rather than searching for one that will meet your needs, is easier.

The intent of this chapter is to encourage you to give some thought about how to start a writing group of your own by telling the story of how my writing group started and how it evolved. You'll learn about the initial concerns we had as we were just getting started and how we addressed our issues over time. You'll gain insight about topics we wrote about and the genres we experimented with. You'll gain an appreciation of the powerful role a writing group can play in sustaining your new pastime and in cultivating friendships.

My group began the summer after my book *Off to School: A Parent's-Eye View of the Kindergarten Year* was published. The collection of letters that I wrote to my son and to his teacher during the course of his kindergarten year eventually materialized into a book. Initially my words were a gift to his teacher. Four years later, after considerably more work, the National Association for the Education of Young Children published *Off to School*. A wonderful editor at NAEYC saw its potential as a contribution to early childhood education and to the importance of teacher/parent communication.

Although I hardly considered myself a writer at that time, I had several friends who tried to foist that distinction on me after they had read my book. They told me on various occasions that they often had the desire to write. Many confessed to having started and abandoned more than just a few blank journals over the years. Others suggested that if I started a writing group, and invited them to join, they might be inspired to do more writing. With that vote of confidence, I invited six women to my home one day in the middle of July. I had no idea what I was doing.

Dear Friends,

I am starting a writing group (for lack of a better name) this summer and thought you might like to come. We'll meet from 10 am – noon on July 2nd and August 5th. We'll use our time together to write, to share ideas about what to write, and to give each other feedback and encouragement. If this idea sounds appealing to you, then please come to my home with pen, paper, and your own expectations. If you've written something you'd like to share, then bring it along. Of course, there will be refreshments. Everyone knows that you can't write without eating and/or drinking something!

Hope to see you.
Irene

Everyone came on that sunny summer morning, toting their bags of journals and notebooks. Jenn even came with her newborn daughter. I helped her set up Avery's portacrib in an upstairs bedroom and, with all the confidence I could muster, reassured her that Avery would indeed cooperate by taking her expected nap. I thought back to my days as a new mom and wondered if I would have been as determined as Jenn was to commit herself to joining a writing group. What I was convinced of, however, was that her daughter would provide a great deal of raw material for her writing. In fact, at the end of the summer, we all vowed to make time in our datebooks for monthly meetings, even though we were all working full time. We all had children in our lives and busy schedules.

I remember being somewhat apprehensive several times during the first year that, despite everyone's best intentions, the group was just not going to work. Indeed, attendance at our meetings fluctuated a great deal. Still, enough of us were committed to keeping the group going. We never canceled a meeting. We met in order to establish a predictable routine. We figured that when others had time, our group would be waiting for them. Luckily, at least two or three people brought writing to share. While not everyone was writing as much as they would have liked, everyone agreed that if it weren't for the group they would be writing even less or not at all. A painfully honest group we were and still are.

"I wrote this *for* the group," Martha or Carol or Jenn or Kristen or Polly or Sue would say before sharing their piece. At first, I have to admit, I found this statement to be very disconcerting, for I wanted everybody to be motivated to write primarily for themselves. How could they not understand that? I had forgotten how long it had taken me before I was motivated to write. When I found *myself* saying to a writing group member prior to a meeting, "So, did you write anything *for* the group?" I realized I was doing exactly what I criticized my friends for doing. As each meeting date approached, I always worried that no one would bring any writing to share. Eventually, I realized this rarely happened because the writing group provided the motivation for members to write. Our members now say they write *because* of the group. What a difference a word makes.

Although it took considerable time alone for me to establish the habit of writing, the time came when I started to crave some companionship. You may be at that point right now or will be at some point in the near future, and for very good reason. You may wish to compare notes with others who are trying their hand at writing. You may want to know how others find the time to write or what writing routines work for them. You might be interested in what motivates others to write and how they manage to sustain their routines. Of course you've got to be curious about what they're writing and how they get ideas. And maybe—just maybe—you've written something that you'd like to read to others just to get their reaction. You may also be getting such pleasure out of writing yourself that you'd like to encourage others to do the same.

Are you becoming a writer? What else would you call yourself if you do indeed cart around a small notebook in your pocket and manage to find the time to write? Perhaps you've discovered that your word photos have increased in number and you may have committed yourself to a daily routine. Perhaps you've even transformed one or more into a longer, more polished piece of writing. And, how about that collection of blank journals that used to haunt you? I'll bet one has become your favorite journal now. You may have written on many pages and some may have special mementos affixed to them. What do you make of all this?

I suggest that you embrace your new identity. Admit to a friend or two that you've started writing. Perhaps you can acknowledge that journaling has become a regular habit. If you take a calculated risk and find the *right* friends to tell, you might be pleasantly surprised that you are not alone. After all, *someone* must be buying all those journals and notebooks that you see for sale in so many locations. Some friends may be thrilled to learn that they are no longer alone, in their solitary pastime, and may be very willing to join with you to form a writing group. I did it and you can too. You could even use this book as a guide.

During the first year that my writing group met, we always debated about what we were going to write. A few members subscribed to the idea of discovering their own topics, while others liked the idea of having a common assignment. One of our first successful assignments was for everyone to find a special object that reminded us of a memory. Kristen wrote about a string of pearls. Jenn wrote about her daughter Avery's tiny disposable diaper. Polly wrote about some Mexican dolls. Martha wrote about a cross, and I wrote about my dog Spody's identification tag, which I still had on my key ring many years after she had died. As we listened to the memories evoked by our assortment of special objects, we realized that learning about our friends' lives through their words was so much fun. Having the opportunity to wrestle with the same self-imposed assignment engendered a spirit of camaraderie and community. We also discovered, over time, that there was no limit to what we could write about!

As the years went on, however, group-imposed assignments were less useful. This serves to reaffirm my belief in the value of coming up with your own ideas by snapping a word photo or jotting down an entry in your writer's notebook or journal. If you decide to start your own writing group, and you've had success with these techniques, invite others to experiment with them. Just as a common assignment can generate a worthwhile discussion, experimenting with a favorite strategy can serve a similar purpose. The benefit of either approach will be the inspiration that will come from hearing what others have written. As we grow to read like writers, we also start listening to the work of others in the same way.

When members of my writing group listen to the pieces others share, they can't help but make a personal connection that often moves them to write a piece of their own. For example, when Edie wrote about a trip to her childhood home, I suddenly longed to put into words the feelings I had when I recently visited mine. Polly's piece about her daughter leaving for college inspired others to think of poignant departures in their own lives. When Jenn wrote about her growing family, Martha realized her five grandsons were potential raw material for her own extended family stories.

In time we also had extensive debates about what form our writing should take, and that continues to this day. While some members initially had fantasies of writing novels and children's books, we soon understood that this was an unrealistic expectation until we had much more experience writing. In addition, as we spent more time reading about writing and talking about writing, we realized what a complicated craft it is. For this reason, we saw the value in exploring shorter and more manageable forms—letters, anecdotes, essays, and poems. Manageable does not necessarily mean easier, however. Letter writing, for example, proved to be a very accessible and satisfying form. Penny, Polly, and I often wrote letters to the editor of the local newspaper on topics about which we felt passionate. Although not all were published, we never regretted having written them because we felt the satisfaction that comes from clarifying our opinions. Many of us even enjoyed writing letters we knew we would never send, because writing helped us sort through our feelings. Many members also realized that letter writing enabled them to discover their authentic voices.

Journal writing was another legitimate form of writing that gave our members the opportunity to write freely. Over the years, many joined me in sharing selected excerpts from their journals at our writing group meetings. Although our journal entries were not polished pieces, they often represented the only writing we could manage to do while we were working full time. This was especially true for me the first year I became a principal. If I hadn't been able to read excerpts from my journal, I would have had nothing to share at our monthly meetings. Journal writing also proved to be a useful form of writing for those embarking on new ventures—becoming grandparents, exploring new hobbies, traveling, and even transitioning to retirement.

I continue to think that journal entries are a legitimate form of writing to share. Often an entry, or even an excerpt will illuminate an observation or a feeling or an insight that actually does mean something of consequence for the writer. If a writing group is composed of friends who care about one another, reading a journal entry helps people get to know one another more intimately. Indeed, we discovered that hearing each other's journal entries did just that. It strengthened our group.

This pattern of genuinely caring about what each of us wrote helped to sustain the group over time. While each of us admitted in our most upbeat and confident moments that we wrote for our own amusement, we were all pleased when our words resonated with others. Indeed our efforts then took on added value when our lead sentence or bits of dialogue over which we had agonized or our intentional choice of words made an impression on others. Likewise, when a group member pointed out a quality about our writing that we had not fully intended, we gained more confidence in our ability.

Many members often mentioned another reason why the writing group was so valuable. Showing up each month imposed a deadline. The deadline was not because we wanted to publish and needed feedback on our work, although we certainly offered feedback when members asked for it. But the primary purpose for joining a writing group, as you are growing into your new role as a writer, is to keep you writing! Knowing that you have a meeting to attend with others, who look forward to hearing what you've written, is the kind of motivation you can't manufacture if you're working all by yourself. Writing for an audience also forces everyone to set a higher standard for themselves. They want to be understood by others and, as a result, pay more attention to their clarity of expression.

As our writing group gave us more confidence in our writing ability, some of us started taking workshops offered at area colleges or community education programs. These opportunities provided us with experiences to hone our skills and to work with individuals who could provide us with more critical feedback. Others finally felt more comfortable perusing the writing section of the local library or bookstore and the collection of books intrigued them. Still others sought out periodicals dedicated to the writer's craft. While the magazines were aimed at professional writers, often these articles would benefit our group and we shared them with one another. Over the years, our group needed to be able to sustain writers of all levels of ability.

The logistics of facilitating a writing group are fairly simple. From the very beginning, we met once a month for two hours, which was sufficient time for members to read their work. Each writer was responsible for letting everyone else know the kind of feedback they desired. This allowed the writer to be in control. We also reserved time for members to initiate a discussion about the writing process and to raise questions that were troubling them. We met at a different member's home each month as a way for everyone to feel involved. The member who hosted the meeting also provided simple refreshments.

Since the group was my idea, I have always assumed the role of facilitator and this may be the role that you take on as well. I signal the official start of each meeting, make announcements, and distribute any relevant handouts. I ask who has brought a piece of writing to share and suggest the order in which to proceed to ensure that everyone has sufficient time. Finally, I send out an email reminder following each meeting, noting the next meeting date and location.

In short, starting a writing group is a relatively simple matter. All you need are a few friends who wish they could make more time to write, a comfortable place to meet, and some refreshments. Sustaining a writing group over time, though, is a much more challenging endeavor. I know this firsthand for I have joined and quit many writing groups in my time. This particular writing group is different and periodically I ask my friends why they think it works. At one meeting Penny, who was not one of the original members, put her thoughts down in a letter that she wrote to our group a few years after joining. She said:

> It is the generous spirit of this particular group that keeps me coming. In our small circle we can say whatever we damn well want however we damn well please. We don't have to worry about whether anyone else would want to read it, whether it's "good," whether it's publishable—we just do it for the sheer joy of putting one word after another in the rhythm of our own inner voices, the very rhythms of our voices expressing our sensibility about the world, about ourselves, about the nature of existence.

Edie who, like Penny, has found the letter to be a very useful if under-appreciated literary form penned the following letter to our group:

I sit here now surrounded by a motley collection of spiral binders, loose papers, notebooks and journals holding years worth of writing and I am grateful to you. I would never have done any of this without you, my audience and my inspiration, both critic and coach. You have been the reason to record a random thought. You have been the deadline to deliver a coherent passage. You have been the safe haven for sharing the hard times. But in the sharing, those hard times grew easier to bear. And in the sharing the good times and memories became even more precious.

The right kind of writing group is one that will keep you writing. It will also enable you to enjoy writing as a pleasurable pastime in the company of others who might grow to be your treasured friends. A writing group provides a safe and receptive audience and the camaraderie that is necessary to sustain your habit. When you have the opportunity to read your piece aloud to others and you hear laughter at a spot that you hoped was funny, you gain confidence in your writing ability. When you sense that others were touched by your choice of words and the emotions they evoked, you start to believe in yourself. While writing may always be a pastime fraught with insecurity and self-doubt, the inspiration that comes from participating in a writing group is well worth the commitment.

Does Starting a Writing Group Make Sense?

1. Have you been writing on a regular basis?

If writing is slowly but surely becoming habit forming, then you have a new hobby. You've discovered the pleasure of writing to record an experience you want to remember, to reflect on a situation you've encountered, or to think through a problem in order to reach a solution. This is not to say that writing comes as easily to you as you'd like, or that you have set your sights on publishing. Rather, you've been making time to write on a regular basis and no longer consider it a waste of time. Writing is a useful and satisfying part of your life.

2. Do you worry that you may not be able to sustain your habit over time?

Given the busy lives we lead, with so many competing demands, sustaining our writing habit may be difficult. Without deadlines or assignments or projects that *need* to be done, writing hobbyists may want to consider imposing their own deadlines. A writing group that meets on a regular basis provides a built-in deadline.

3. Do you wish you had others with whom you could talk about writing?

As is true with anyone starting a new endeavor, getting to know other like-minded individuals who are excited about their new interest is often helpful. You might want to compare notes about how others find the time to write or what writing routines work for them. You might be interested in what others write about and how they get ideas. Even though you've been writing for your own amusement, you may very well have written something that you'd like to share with another person who can appreciate what you're trying to say. Writing can be a lonely pursuit. Since writing groups for novice writers can be hard to find, this could be the best reason to start one yourself!

CHAPTER EIGHT

What's Publication All About?

In every real sense, the writer writes in order to teach himself,
to understand himself, to satisfy himself;
the publishing of his ideas is a curious anticlimax.
—**Alfred Kazin**

Although writing for publication is not the ultimate goal for those of us who simply want to write for pleasure, at some point we may have the desire to "do something" with some of our words. The purpose of this chapter is to broaden the concept of publication beyond that of a traditional publisher. We will explore the endless ways of creating "gifts of words" as satisfying forms of publishing for ourselves and for others. This chapter will highlight a few in order to inspire you to design gifts of your own.

As we've already mentioned in the last chapter, being a member of a writing group offers an immediate opportunity for a less conventional form of publishing that serves an important purpose. Having a monthly meeting to attend, with the expectation that you will read a piece of writing, provides an incentive to revisit your draft with a more critical eye. You want your piece to be understood so you try harder to clarify your meaning. You may have written an anecdote, which upon rereading brings back a fond memory and you are eager to share it with your friends. You may say to yourself, as do many of my writing group members, "Hey, I'm so glad I wrote that!" Sharing it forges a connection that enriches relationships and inspires others to write about similar experiences they suddenly remember.

After our writing group had been meeting for three years, Polly suggested that we make a collection of our favorite pieces. She proposed that we have a writing swap at our final meeting of the year. We asked each member to select one or two of their favorites and make enough copies for everyone. The only requirement was that it should be printed on a standard 8.5 x 11 hole-punched sheet of paper. Everybody was responsible for bringing a loose-leaf binder. We placed our contributions on a long table and, in assembly-line fashion, members took a copy from each pile. We affectionately called our notebook *Circle of Pens*. It was such a good idea!

"Hey, I remember that poem about Uncle Cecil," Carol exclaimed to Polly when she spotted the following poem.

Uncle Cecil
by Polly Attwood

We had a postcard
from Uncle Cecil
Having a fine old time
in Australia.
He had decided to take a cruise
from his LA mobile home.
Incredible old man.

Two days later
a phone call
from his neighbor.

An accident?
Yes, on the way home
in a taxi from the ship
Broken bones, internal injuries
A coma.
Then he died.

He would have been
ninety-seven
next
week.

"And Carol, I'm so glad you included the letter you wrote about that wonderful class you were so attached to," Polly said with a smile.

"And there's 'Found Food'!" I said to Edie. "I'm so glad to have my own copy."

Dear Fifth-Grade Teacher
by Carol Birdsall

You'll soon receive,
Under separate cover, I believe,
Some young humans marked
Fragile – Handle with care,
Attached, herewith, I have for you,
Some guidelines for this happy crew.

They know their facts, I say with pride.
Just watch 'em multiply and divide.
They read well and widely on their own,
When forced to stop they tend to groan.

To charm them into utter euphoria,
Read aloud from almost any story—
A tale of treasure or Louisa May,
You'll enchant them if possible, every day?

They create beauty, in writing and in art,
And to be sure, it comes from the heart.
Oh, one hundred eighty days is not enough!
Parting with these friends of mine is rough.
I loved them dearly while they were my guests,
But little birds must leave their nests.

Found Food
by Edie Lipinski

Melt, shred, slice, grind,
Peel, chop, dice, combine.

Apple, scrapple, fig and ham,
Succotash, a can of spam.

Hazelnuts, mayonnaise,
Á la king, Hollandaise.

Fry, broil, bake, sauté,
Simmer, grill, poach, flambé.

Tuna, turkey, turnips, torte,
Sherry, vodka, wine and port.

Garnish, sprinkle, season, chill,
Add the tarragon and dill.

Pastry, parsley, pilaf, prune,
Cauliflower, macaroon.

Cover, freeze, wrap tightly, store.
Best if made the night before.

Everyone was thrilled to discover that so many of our old favorites were now ours to reread at our leisure. We had a hunch the tradition was worth continuing and every few years we vowed to add to our notebooks. We also found that the *Circle of Pens* was beneficial when we welcomed new members to our group. Our sampling of work about a variety of topics—food, holidays, parents, parenting, people, places, pets, school, travel, and technology—enabled new members to get acquainted with us through our writing.

A few years after compiling *Circle of Pens*, I decided to take another loose-leaf notebook and make a book of my own writing that I had completed over the years. Scattered in various locations around my house were anecdotes, poems, essays, and letters. I found some tucked away in folders in a file cabinet in the basement. Still others, actual articles that had been published in magazines, were in a pile on a bookshelf in my study. I found a few pieces that were not quite finished still on my computer. Gathering everything together took a while, but having all my writing in one place felt good.

Eventually I decided to organize the notebook of writing by genre—anecdotes, poems, essays, letters, articles, and even short stories. Unlike *Circle of Pens*, mine remains nameless, but I did slip a postcard behind the plastic sleeve on the front cover with the following quote: "Every single moment you are writing the story of your life." While my notebook certainly did contain some published articles, the majority of pieces were for my eyes only. I considered the notebook a gift to myself.

Sometimes writing that starts out for yourself is worthy of a larger audience. Sometimes you know it; other times a friend with whom you've shared your words tells you. I often take on this role, as an unofficial agent, for some of my unassuming writing group members. As is the case with publishing, the key is to find just the right venue to showcase their efforts. When I became an elementary school principal, I was very proud to "publish" poems that two of my writing group members wrote.

I featured Jenn's poem called "Lost and Found" at my school, beside the clothing rack and shelf that held an assortment of sweatshirts, jackets, lunch boxes, and boots.

Lost and Found
by Jenn Eisenheim

Jackets, wallets, rings and gloves,
Mittens, scarves that once were loved
The boot you thought was gone forever,
Thinking you would find it never.

A lunch box filled with last week's meal,
That now has lost all its appeal.
They call these items Lost and Found,
As they pile high upon this mound.

If these items belong to you,
Then take them home and do this too
Take a marker, or needle and thread,
Write, stitch or carve your name in red.

And in the future, make sure and be
More careful of your things, you see—
For once the pile begins to grow,
It's hard to stop it – this we know.

When our PTO decided to publish a school cookbook, I thought "Found Food" by Edie would be a fitting addition. I submitted it on behalf of Edie and the parent who edited the cookbook couldn't have been happier.

I was probably the first member of my writing group to experiment with the idea of using my words as a gift to someone. The idea was the result of my having a fairly extensive stockpile of writing from which to choose. My first gift of words, which I described in chapter five, was initially a thank you present to Mary Yardley, my son's kindergarten teacher. Four years later, the book was formally published.

My next effort was a one-of-a kind publication that I made for my son Ted when he graduated from high school. The idea occurred to me several years before his graduation when I realized how many entries in my writer's notebook were about him.

April 23 — I have to admit, that in my mind at least, a new writing project is in the works, which I'm hoping to give to Ted when he graduates from high school. Bob will probably try to talk me out of it as much as my female friends, who are mothers, have been encouraging me to do it. Nevertheless, I've got to do it so I'm hoping Ted will receive it in the spirit in which it is being given. He often teases me about all the writing I do in my little notebooks so now he's going to have a chance to read a small sampling.

As it turned out, Ted did appreciate my gift. I didn't present it to him in June when he graduated from high school, though. I waited until September, when just the two of us were at home alone. We were actually sitting in the living room talking about his upcoming trip to Clark University where he was headed in a few days.

"So Ted," I stammered. "I made something for you for graduation but

I didn't know when a good time would be to give it to you. Dad wasn't sure about the idea, so maybe that's part of my hesitation." Ted looked at me quizzically as my words just gushed out all in one breath. "It's something I made for you but I had so much fun doing it and I'd be happy to keep it if you think it's really silly and it won't hurt my feelings."

He had no idea what I was talking about, but he noticed I was holding something behind my back. I hadn't even wrapped it because I didn't want to make a big deal out of my present. I put the slim journal into Ted's hands.

"Go ahead. Open it," I said as I kept talking. "You've always been curious about what I write in all my little notebooks and have often teased me about them. Well, now you're going to see." He flipped through the book. The photos captured his attention first.

"I remember making that huge city with all the boxes and roads," he said. "And there's Stuart and me going to baseball camp. How did you do this?" he asked before he noticed my organizational scheme—"Pastimes and Play, Bowman Elementary School, Holidays, Clarke Middle School, Vacations, Lexington High School." He smiled as he spotted familiar candid photos as well as the wallet size school pictures that marked his progression from kindergarten through twelfth grade. Before long, the writing captured his attention too. I had revised, edited, typed, and glued onto the blank pages a small number of carefully selected and revised entries that spanned Ted's school years. The following, written several years apart, were from "Pastimes and Play."

September 27 — Since Wednesday you had been talking about a fair you were having on Sunday at 11 am. Dad and I were not quite sure what to make of this, not quite believing that your plan was going to materialize. On Sunday, while we rushed around getting the house ready for a visit from Grandma, you prepared the yard for the fair. Suddenly we heard voices in the backyard and when we looked out the window we saw Tracy, Russell, Ryan, Tyler, Jay, Aruna, Ram, Sean, Kasey, and Jesse. You came in and announced, "I think the fair is starting. Everyone is in the backyard." Your magic show was one of your best. You did the nickel in the box, the shell trick, and the card trick. What a success!

July 8 — A swarm of white t-shirts and assorted baseball capped boys gather under an old oak tree in the middle of a manicured field. It's the closing meeting where the commissioner a.k.a. Eddie Gallagher holds forth before this week's campers with talk about baseball and lessons for life. You've had two weeks at Belmont Hill and each day you arrive home enthusiastic and energized by your experience. News of how many singles, doubles, and triples you've gotten during the games and the different kinds of slides you've practiced fill you with a feeling of such pride and accomplishment.

Ted's reaction couldn't have been more perfect and I breathed a sigh of relief. After looking at the collage of photos I had placed on the first page and then quickly flipping through the journal, he immediately realized what this gift was all about.

"How could you think I wouldn't like this, Mom?" he said. "This is the story of my life!"

Over the years, I've made quite a few gifts of words from selected entries in my word photo notebooks. As the one-year anniversary of my sister's death approached, I decided that it might be comforting for me to have a collection of my word photos of her all in one place. At first it was going to be a gift to myself. As I worked on it, I decided that it would also be a present I could give to Ellie's best friend. Unlike the one-of-kind book for my son, which included photos, this one had "clip-art" illustrations. Fifty-one word photos and accompanying illustrations filled a twenty-two-page booklet that I had printed at local copy shop.

Since that first book, I've gone on to make two additional gifts taken from my notebook of PHOTOS That Have Never Been Taken. One was a thank you present I gave to two parents just before my retirement. The booklet contained sixteen snapshots that captured the ups and downs of the building project they facilitated following a fire that destroyed our playground. As was the case with my first booklet, I had no idea when I was writing my word photos that I would use them for this purpose.

My most recent gift of words was a birthday present I gave to another special individual whom I met in a poetry group the year after I retired. Despite our thirty-year difference in age, we became good friends. On the occasion of her 94th birthday, I presented her with a booklet of thirty-seven "photos" I had captured with my pen during the first year of our friendship. Once again, the project emerged because I happened to have the raw material.

January 8 "Driving Jan to Robbins Library" — Who would have thought I'd be in a poetry class with Jan Slepian, the author of *The Hungry Thing*, one of my favorite children's books when I was teaching second grade? Today I gave her a lift to our poetry class. Maybe I'll get to know her.

June 27 "Sitting with Jan on the bike path behind Sunrise" — Jan was on her motorized scooter she calls Joey. I sat on a bench. Jan reached into her basket and pulled out a new poem she's been working on and started talking about how it started, why it draws her in, and what form it might take. I love when she lets me in on her thinking.

December 30 "Having tea with Jan at her table" — As we neared the end of 2014 Jan asked me what were the important events in my life during this past year. Of course Jan probably knew the publication of *A Principal's Journey* was one such event but the very next thought that occurred to me was my getting to know Jan. She smiled when I said that because that too was one of her most memorable events in addition to her joining the poetry group.

Capturing word photos has appealed to others with whom I've worked in the workshops and courses I've taught over the years. What amazes me is the many different kinds of gifts individuals can make once they have sufficient raw material. Gemma, a young mother from Catalonia, decided to compile a series of anecdotes to accompany the many real photos she took during the time she lived in Lexington, Massachusetts. She and her husband returned to Spain with a wonderful collection of photo-enhanced reminiscences. Gemma's piece and the word photos of many others with whom I have worked are included in chapter ten.

I am convinced that at every stage of our lives we can find reasons to write. We can then make personal gifts of words that are satisfying forms of publication. Parents of any age, who discover the benefits of writing, preserve memories for themselves as well as for their children. Grandparents who spend time with their grandchildren can craft a gift of words for their own children.

Individuals who travel and find time to jot down their reflections along the way create a gift for themselves as well as for their traveling companions. We can use the raw material in our journals, writer's notebooks, and word photo collections to create greeting cards, letters, poems, anecdotes, and essays. Most of the time, the gifts are modest in size and in scope, which makes them manageable to complete. But once in while, I must admit, a bigger project can emerge. Such a project surfaced the summer after my retirement. Although my decision to retire came at exactly the right time, I anticipated that I would need some sort of transition to a new way of life. I turned to writing to help me make this transition and my efforts resulted in a book called *A Principal's Journey: The School as My Classroom.*

This project afforded me the opportunity to reflect on my twelve years as an elementary school principal. It was a role that I would never have imagined pursuing at the start of my career, but when I turned fifty I decided to give it a try. In fact, the kind of principal I tried to be was one who viewed the school through the eyes of a teacher. Through a series of candid and thoughtful essays, my book told the story of what can happen when a principal brings to her job the heart and mindset of an effective teacher. Eventually I decided to seek a broader audience through publication. My dedication served as a thank you present to the entire school community.

For my staff at South Row School
For my colleagues in the Chelmsford Public Schools
And, for my students and their families
all of whom helped me to become
the kind of principal
I wanted to be

By broadening the concept of publication to include the variety of personal gifts of words discussed in this chapter, we novice writers can reap many benefits. As we discover a potential audience for our writing, we create a need to revise and fine tune our work. The clarity of our expression becomes a stronger goal because others will read our words and we want to be sure that we are understood. Finally, when we take a risk and "do something with our words" and receive an appreciative response, we will be motivated to keep writing.

Making a Gift of Words

I. Periodically make time to reread your journals, your word photo notebooks, and your writer's notebooks.

A gift of words can only be made after you've amassed a fair amount of writing. Make time to reread what you've written with an eye toward recognizing recurring subjects, ideas, and themes. As you're reviewing your journals, you may need to develop a system for noting where similar ideas have occurred. Color-coded post-it flags are useful to tag similar entries. The goal initially is to locate potential material.

2. Decide who will be a worthwhile recipient of your words.

While it is very gratifying to give a gift to another person, never rule out the possibility that making a gift for yourself is an excellent place to start. You may have discovered some good ideas that you now have a desire to develop into a more polished piece of writing just for yourself. On the other hand, you may also have writings about people or events that you believe deserve a broader audience. The potential audience is limitless and may include your friends, children, grandchildren, parents, grandparents, and even colleagues at work. Be sure to select an appreciative recipient.

3. Consider the form your writing might take.

Letters are a terrific form of writing and, with their built in audience in mind, your voice as a writer will emerge. Several entries in your journal or writer's notebook may be appropriate for an anecdote or an essay. Some of your jottings may be just right for a poem. You may have an occasion to deliver your words orally at a retirement party, a wedding reception, or even a memorial service. Words from the heart are appreciated. Don't be surprised if someone asks you for a copy.

4. Decide how BIG a gift of words is reasonable.

Don't set yourself up for failure! Making a gift of any kind is a labor of love and a gift of words is going to take some work. Transforming your words into a greeting card for a loved one will be easier than amassing a series of word photos that will remind your family of their summer vacation. Considering whether or not photos will accompany your words will inform your decision about what your finished product will look like. Will it be handwritten or typed? Will it be a one-of-a-kind project or one that can be photocopied?

5. Consider the time and place for your presentation.

By the time you finish making your gift, you may find it hard to part with it. As is true with any gift, you can't really be sure how it will be received. If you've selected your recipient with care and considered an appropriate time and place for your presentation, chances are that you will be as thrilled by their reaction as they are with your gift.

CHAPTER NINE

How Are You Going to Keep Growing as a Writer?

We are all apprentices in a craft where no one ever becomes a master.
—Ernest Hemingway

Now that you've made it to this second to last chapter, I have a hunch you've been successfully experimenting with various ways to make writing a pleasurable pastime. You may now have a journal in which you write on a regular basis. Note that I did not say every day, because by now you've understood the value in setting realistic expectations. Perhaps the idea of free writing in a writer's notebook has been an appealing strategy. You may now take great pride in flipping through your notebook and recognizing some common themes or kernels of ideas that you could transform into an anecdote, a letter, or a poem. You may have snapped enough word photos to fill a small notebook.

Write On! has been about expanding your understanding of what the writing process entails and encouraging you to find ways to experience it. It has been about inviting you to consider writing as an enjoyable hobby. It has been about experiencing writing as a tool for self-discovery, reflection, and amusement. It has been about realizing that writing can be a tool for problem solving. It has been about seeing writing as a means to achieve mindfulness. Now that you have more confidence in your ability to write, you realize how much more you have to learn. In this chapter, we will focus on next steps for you to think about in order to continue to grow as a writer. The first involves additional reading to deepen and broaden your understanding of the writing process. The second is to stress the value of finding workshops and courses led by instructors who will offer assistance based on your needs and nudge you in new directions.

We'll begin first with a selection of books that I have gradually accumulated over the years. I turn to them on a regular basis to nourish and to inspire me. Although they are books written by professional writers, we hobbyists *must* begin to read books about writing if we are to continue to learn and grow.

The first book is Anne Lamott's classic, *Bird by Bird: Some Instructions on Writing and Life.* It is one of the funniest books I've ever read about writing. In *Bird by Bird*, Lamott promotes the importance of always seeking to tell the truth when you write. Drawing from her own life, she strives to make sense of her experiences in an honest, irreverent, and self-deprecating style that is her trademark. She reveals numerous truths about writing—that it's hard, messy work, and that writing a "shitty" first draft is about the best you can hope for when you're just starting a piece. She believes in giving yourself short, focused assignments and not having publishing as your ultimate goal.

Dani Shapiro's book, *Still Writing: The Perils and Pleasures of a Creative Life*, sits on my bookshelf right next to *Bird by Bird* and I consider it to have some similar qualities. Shapiro boldly states in her introduction: "...everything you need to know about life can be learned from a genuine and ongoing attempt to write." Unlike Lamott's book, which is divided into five parts with clearly delineated chapters, Shapiro's book reads like a memoir. Her short reflections are summed up in single words or phrases, which can't help but pique your curiosity. She begins with "Scars," which reveals that she was an only child of older parents. She thinks that her lonely, isolated childhood may very well have drawn her to writing. In "Riding the Wave," she offers advice about how to avoid procrastination. "Inner Censor" quite rightly reveals all the worries that everyone has when they sit down to write. She also offers strategies for dealing with them. The short sections that provide digestible information are so much fun to read. This book inspired me to make marginal notes, as if I were engaged in a conversation with the author.

Peter Elbow's book, *Writing With Power: Techniques for Mastering the Writing Process* is also worth checking out, especially if you've found free writing to be a useful strategy. While I just briefly addressed this concept in chapter one, so much more can be learned from Peter Elbow. He begins with a review of the writing process, which will be familiar to you, but he goes into more depth. He reinforces the value of using writing as a tool to discover meaning. He extends the concept of free writing and directed free writing with a number of specific procedures for you to try out. His table of contents includes chapters on revision, audience, feedback, and voice. They are filled with practical and generous advice.

Georgia Heard's book, *Writing Toward Home: Tales and Lessons to Find Your Way* is a wonderful collection of brief thought-provoking vignettes about writing. She, too, emphasizes the value of drawing from one's own experiences for ideas and she offers specific assignments to help you. She describes each assignment with sufficient detail and clarity, inviting experimentation. Her assignments can be personalized in a manner that makes the idea an authentic one for the writer. Georgia Heard reinforces the idea of maintaining a notebook and finding just the right one that will keep you writing. She also suggests experimenting with various locations where you feel comfortable writing.

Breathing In, Breathing Out: Keeping a Writer's Notebook by Ralph Fletcher is a gold mine of information about another technique that will be familiar to you. If keeping a writer's notebook has become one of your habits, then *Breathing In, Breathing Out* will give you more ideas to stretch your thinking and make the most of your entries. I love that Ralph Fletcher is not apologetic about writing in the first person. I found myself not only underlining sentences that were meaningful to me, but also making marginal notes as if I were engaged in a conversation with him. The first half of the book is filled with ideas that help us to be on the lookout for images, insights, observations, and even overheard conversations that are worth remembering. The later portion delves into possible ways to use the entries to craft pieces that beg to be written.

Donald Murray is another author well worth reading, and he has many books to his credit. I believe *Crafting a Life in Essay, Story, Poem* is particularly useful. His two introductory chapters provide an excellent pep talk about what's involved in cultivating a writing habit and in developing the kind of attitude toward your work that will keep you writing. He reinforces the idea of using writing to discover meaning. He advises us not to be dismayed if we don't know ahead of time exactly where our writing may lead.

Murray intentionally titles the next three chapters in a style that invites the reader to "try on" the essay, the story, and the poem. He breaks down each genre into manageable chunks and discusses topics that are critical for crafting a satisfying piece of writing—lead sentences, point- of-view, voice, use of detail, word choice, dialogue, rhythm, and "show, don't tell." He even shares examples of his drafts with revisions he has made. Donald Murray also writes as if he were talking with you, as he generously reveals what he knows about writing in a clear and concise manner.

The next book I'd recommend is another classic, *Writing Down the Bones: Freeing the Writer Within* by Natalie Goldberg. What's distinctive about Goldberg's book is her interest in connecting Zen meditation and writing, as well as her commitment to showing us how much fun writing can be. Her sixty short chapters about writing can be picked up and read in any order. In fact, this book is probably not one that you'd want to pick up and read right through from beginning to end, but one to pick up when you need a little motivation. Some of her chapter titles give you a very good idea of what the focus will be: "Be Specific; Don't Tell, but Show; The Action of a Sentence." Others, however, will pique your curiosity: "Fighting Tofu; Writing is Not a McDonald's Hamburger; One Plus One Equals a Mercedes-Benz." While Goldberg's book is not the book to consult if you are looking for specific guidance on crafting a piece, it does offer many suggestions to get your creative juices flowing.

Stephen King's book *On Writing* is also a wonderful memoir. His life is inextricably linked to writing. The first part tells the story of his early years beginning with his childhood and continuing with his struggle to make it as a writer. Much of it is very entertaining. The middle of the book, a section he describes as a toolbox, is the meatiest part the book. Although it is not a technical guide on how to be a better writer, he covers topics that are important for those who want to write fiction—dialogue, description, and character development. He reinforces the importance of vocabulary and grammar, and reveals his own biases when it comes to writing. He emphasizes the need to be a reader if you want to be a writer.

The Elements of Style by Strunk and White must also be on your bookshelf. It contrasts sharply with all the other books I've mentioned and, at just eighty-five pages, could be considered a quick read. Although it's not the kind of book you cuddle up with, *The Elements of Style* is an essential reference to the basic rules of our English language. A short section includes eleven important principles of composition. Three of my favorites are: "Using the Active Voice; Using Definite, Specific and Concrete Language; and Omitting Needless Words." Every time I read this section, I realize how many other books on writing draw from Strunk and White. I also appreciate how clearly they write as they model the overriding principle of what effective writing should be. Two very practical sections concern matters of form and commonly misused words and expressions.

The final section of *Elements* concerns writing style. I would imagine this part was risky to write, since every writer develops his or her own distinctive style. For this reason, the twenty-one ideas presented are listed as "suggestions." Each is stated as a brief assertion followed by a short elaboration. My favorites include the following: "Write in a way that comes naturally; Work from a suitable design; Write with nouns and verbs; Revise and rewrite; Avoid the use of qualifiers; Avoid fancy words; Be clear." This is not just a book for professional writers, but rather a book for anyone who writes.

Good Prose by Tracy Kidder and Richard Ford would be another good addition to your writing library, if you're interested in writing non-fiction. You may even be familiar with some of Kidder's other books—*The Soul of a New Machine, House,* and *Among School Children._Good Prose* is part memoir as Kidder describes his literary career as a freelance writer for *The*

Atlantic and part exploration of an important relationship he forged with his editor Richard Ford. For this reason, the book is an unusual mix of advice written from the perspectives of a writer and an editor. The authors touch upon important topics about three forms of non-fiction prose—narratives, essays, and memoirs. Each section is replete with concrete examples from other authors and what they've discovered in the process of writing. The narrative section offers advice on point-of-view, characters, and structure. Their rules for memoir are clear: Say difficult things; Stick to the facts; Be harder on yourself than you are on others. With a bit of self-deprecating humor, they advise the reader to try accepting the fact that you are in part a comic figure. The style of *Good Prose* invites the reader to think much in the same way an editor does.

On Writing Well by William Zinsser also focuses on non-fiction writing, but unlike *Good Prose,* its organization makes it relatively easy to find exactly what you're looking for. Eighteen short chapters cover all the basics. The seven chapters in Part I stress the importance of writing clearly, avoiding jargon and big words, using active verbs, and making the reader think that you enjoyed writing the piece. The remaining chapters that comprise Part II provide guidelines for specific forms of writing—how to craft interviews, travel articles, and memoirs. Zinsser offers advice pertaining to writing about scientific and technical subjects, business, sports, criticism, and humor. His suggestions are applicable to all genres and are relevant to fiction as well as to non-fiction.

Early in the book, on pages ten and eleven of *On Writing Well,* Zinsser shares parts of the final manuscript of his chapter entitled "Simplicity" to show the reader what revision looks like. He maintains that each time he rewrites, his goal is to make what he has written "tighter, stronger and more precise, eliminating every element that is not doing useful work." I return to these pages again and again for a reminder about revision. Seeing how Zinsser de-clutters some of his sentences inspires me to be on the lookout for words in my own sentences that are not necessary. These draft pages illustrate the principle that writing is hard work. Few sentences come out right the first time. If they don't for Zinsser, why should we be surprised that they don't for us?

Roy Peter Clarke's contribution to the field of writing is entitled *Writing Tools.* He makes a case that "tools," not hard and fast rules, are adaptable to many different situations. As with many of the other books mentioned so far, one can pick this up and read a short chapter on a topic that is well defined and practical. Each of the fifty short chapters covers a single principle of effective writing. What is significantly different about Clarke's book, though, is the "workshop" feature he has placed at the end of each chapter. He suggests four or five very short, well-crafted assignments to illustrate the principle discussed in the chapter. He invites the reader to experiment and to learn by doing. Sometimes he suggests that you review a piece of your own writing with an eye toward noting certain principles: "Eliminating unnecessary adjectives and adverbs; Varying the length of your sentences; Using strong verbs; and Choosing precise and specific words." Often he sends you to a newspaper or to your favorite author to look for strong leads, sensory detail, or dialogue.

Like William Zinsser, Roy Peter Clarke also shares with the reader how he has made revisions. On page fifty-three he compares a longer version of "Cut big, then small" with a shorter version, which appears in his book. His workshop assignment asks us whether he has cut something that should have been retained and to defend our reasons for keeping it. Finally, he challenges us to review our own work. He says, "Cut without mercy. Begin with big cuts, then small ones. Count how many words you've saved. Calculate the percentage of the whole. Can you cut fifteen percent?"

Escaping into the Open: The Art of Writing True by Elizabeth Berg is also a book worth reading especially if you've been attracted to the many novels she has to her credit. Reading this book is like having a heart-to-heart talk with a good friend. It is both a personal memoir as well as an invitational and inspirational instruction book about writing. For those who enjoy trying out various warm-up exercises, you would do well to head directly to chapter four entitled "If You're a Man, Be a Woman: Exercises to Unleash Your Creativity." Chapter five suggests ways to put more passion and emotion in your writing, and chapter six discusses techniques for making the transition from non-fiction to fiction. But I think, for the purpose of shedding some light on how to continue to nurture yourself as a writer, two chapters stand out. One is about the wisdom of enrolling in writing classes.

The other is about the merit of joining a writing group.

At the end of most chapters, Berg offers what she describes as "homework." Her assignments are fewer in number than those in *Writing Tools,* but they are every bit as useful. Her finale is a big surprise. For all of us who rightly or wrongly reward ourselves with food at the end of a good workday, you'll be amused to find a collection of ten wonderful recipes. I love to cook and bake and I've tried just about all of them, four of which I make all the time— Blueberry Butter Cake, Honey Whole Wheat Bread, Chicken in Yogurt Tomato Sauce, and Baked Apple Pancake which always hits the spot on a lazy Sunday morning!

I believe my handpicked collection of books, a baker's dozen as it turns out, will nourish you as you continue to make writing a pleasurable part of your life. Each book is passionately written in a style that will engage and inspire you. You'll no doubt have your favorites, as I have mine, but I believe my purposefully selective list is a good start. I also believe the books will give you the confidence you need to enroll in a course or a workshop based on the kind of writing you're interested in pursuing. Memoir and poetry classes are very popular, as are those that focus on transforming non-fiction to fiction or crafting a children's book. Many excellent ones are offered at Community Education Centers and Life Long Learning Institutes.

The biggest challenge in taking a course is to be sure the instructor is a writer as well as a person who can teach. You want to work with someone who will inspire you, share what they know, and keep you writing. You want someone who will offer honest and constructive feedback in a manner that will not overwhelm or discourage you—someone who understands the vulnerability of the student/teacher relationship.

Two of my most demanding instructors, one who taught a memoir course and the other a poetry workshop, are good examples. They always begin their feedback by telling us what "is working" and why. They also expect each participant to offer suggestions to others following the same procedure. While I always find the instructor's feedback the most beneficial, the opportunity to articulate what I am learning as I react to the writing of the other participants is also helpful.

Classes are beneficial in other respects. The instructors whose classes I've found the most valuable offer short, well-defined assignments that provide focus and direction. Models from published writers serve as guides to help us craft our own projects. Writing courses and workshops have inherent deadlines that guard against procrastination. At the end of several sessions, you can look forward to reviewing your revised work, based on the feedback you've received, and deciding for yourself what your next step might be. It may be another course. It may be a new project. An unexpected bonus will be the friends you'll make!

Next Steps to Keep Growing as a Writer

1. Which titles among the baker's dozen interest you the most?

Bird by Bird by Anne Lamott and *Still Writing* by Dani Shapiro would be good choices if you're longing to read more about the connection between writing and life. *Breathing In, Breathing Out* by Ralph Fletcher should go to the top of your list if you've decided you need more guidance in maintaining a writer's notebook. If you've enjoyed the discovery aspect of free writing, Peter Elbow's book *Writing With Power* will offer you more techniques for mastering the writing process. If assignments are what you are craving at this point, then you have many options. Georgia Heard's *Writing Toward Home* provides a number of assignments that will inspire you to draw from your experience. If a creative spark is what you need, Natalie Goldberg's *Writing Down the Bones* will free the writer within you and show how much fun writing can be. Perhaps you've discovered that non-fiction is really where you want to spend more time. Books that offer guidance about crafting essays, memoirs, and personal narratives include *Crafting a Life in Essay, Story, Poem* by Donald Murray and *Good Prose* by Tracy Kidder and Richard Ford.

2. Is there a particular writing genre that you would like to delve into?

Your writer's notebook and journal entries may reveal your interest in a specific writing genre—memoir, essay, poem, personal narrative. If you are interested in a more ambitious genre—a children's book, a mystery, or a screenplay, then this would be the time to check out the writing section in your library or local bookstore for additional resources. While many principles of writing apply to all genres, learning about the structure and conventions of each is useful.

3. Are workshops or courses available in your community?

Community Education Programs as well as Life Long Learning Institutes offer writing courses and workshops on a variety of topics. Peruse their catalogues and see what appeals to you. Get a sense of the qualifications of the instructor by checking out the biographical information that is generally included. A teacher who has expertise in a particular genre will be able to provide the kind of structure and feedback that will enable you to start on a new project with greater confidence than if you were working alone. In addition, you'll meet other workshop participants with whom you can share ideas and information.

CHAPTER TEN

How Can the Writing of Others Inspire You?

When we read the experiences that others have shared,
we are inspired to write our own.
—Irene Hannigan

This last chapter features the writing of some of the people with whom I have worked in various workshops, courses, and writing groups I have facilitated. They have managed to make time to write despite their busy schedules and have experimented with many of the ideas you've read about in this book. They have been willing to share their work in the spirit of inspiring you to take your own next steps. And, yes, they did revise them because they knew you would be reading them!

Read the following word photos and writer's notebook entries as a writer. Is there one that makes you think of an idea that you'd like to write about? Which ones evoke a picture you can imagine? What words or phrases do you especially like? What verbs were well chosen by the author?

WORD PHOTO ENTRIES

Morning Coffee
by Joe Johnston

Each morning I crawl from my warm bed and stumble like a drunk, feeling my way toward the kitchen, where my hand pours 3 two-cup measures of water into a pot sitting on a hot burner. Then 45 grams of ground coffee go into a paper filter in a holder on a carafe. Today it's Kenya AA. In ten minutes the water boils. I pour it on the coffee where it drips slowly. In ten minutes time, nearly all the water has seeped through and I steal a cup. I raise it towards my lips and the aroma fills my brain cavity; my eye twitches. I sip. A lush bright sweet but acidic flavor moves over my tongue bathing it then narrowing to a swallow that warms my throat. Another sip and I open my eyes. I sigh, smile, and ask, "What have you for me... Day?"

Brightening Up a Gray Day
by Margaret Gooch

Rose-colored, like a large open bloom it seemed, held by the woman strolling across the pavement, her gray slacks like the flower's slender stalk. Soon after, a couple dressed in blue and yellow appear, then a man with a yellow-striped jacket accompanied by a little girl dressed in pink happily skipping through puddles. Maybe rain is more likely to draw forth color than the pure cold of snow, when dark-colored garments are the order of the day. This gray day can use some brightness!

WRITER'S NOTEBOOK & JOURNAL ENTRIES

Always Drink Scotch
by Annette Hodess

Pigtails fly as dangling heels hitch onto the silver hoop of the spinning stool as my fingers grasp the red nail headed seat. The whirling world improves the vista of the yacht club bar overlooking the slag and tailings chocked Ohio River. The fiery red smoke of the steel mills boarding the River illuminate the yacht club docks; there are no yachts only small motorboats. The radio cries country music of life gone wrong as I sip Shirley Temples with double cherry stems while elbowed between the stools of Dad and his friend, "Uncle" Sam. The sticky bar glues Dad's short Martell on the rocks and tall, mostly cubes, water glass. Uncle Sam alternates between Scotch and water and a "boilermaker;" a whiskey shot with a beer. With raised caterpillar eyebrows, Uncle Sam leans toward me and whispers, in Marlboro reeked breath, "Always drink Scotch, It won't make you sick."

An Unforgettable Adventure
by Tim Harrington

I've just landed in Thailand after an arduous flight across the Pacific. After cracking open the hatch, I am assaulted by a wave of heat and humidity that nearly takes my breath away. I was expecting the fragrance of local flowers, but that was not to be the case. Instead the smell of rotting vegetation, jet fuel, and hydraulic oil permeated the air. This base was built by the Japanese during World War II and is being upgraded to support our mission against North Vietnam. Indoctrination briefings ensue: snake danger, requirement to drink only Coca Cola and bottled beer because water is not safe, local customs, and finally what to do if shot down in North Vietnam. I found all of this intimidating. I won't fly my first mission until checked out by a pilot who is familiar with the area and procedures. So, I'm about to begin an adventure that I will never forget.

A Virtual Tour of Life
by Judy B. Katz

The wonders of modern technology allow me to take a virtual tour of an estate sale. I am a voyeur into someone else's world from the comfort of my home.

I look at all the finery and think about who lived there and wonder about their life story. I peruse each room and am struck by this life-like time capsule—furnishings and memories created by a family making a house their home. Yet today each object is reduced to the price tag it bears.

Home decor and memories are for sale by those eager to capture and incorporate them into their own home and begin the cycle again. Once eager to be among the treasure hunters, I am now filled with sadness watching a home lose its charm and individuality. I am struck by how this feels reminiscent of becoming an empty nester again only in a much more profound and final way. Someone is not just moving on to college, a job or marriage. There will be no more returning to this nest and the myriad of memories that have constituted a life.

I imagine the sounds of family laughter fading away along with the contents of this home.

What More Could I Ask For?
by Sandra S. Bittenbender

Today I reflect on that December day—the day my daughter was born. Her cries were loud and the bright lights of the delivery room illuminated the roof of her mouth. Her palate was complete and smooth. She would be blessed with the option of perfect speech. Her fingers and toes were all there, ten of each. She was startled by a noise and blinked in a sudden flash of light. She would see and hear the way we all hope. What more could I ask for?

Poetry is a genre that many novice writers have fun experimenting with even before they've taken any courses or workshops specifically dedicated to this genre. Sometimes words simply emerge in a poetic form and satisfy the writer's desire to express an idea that would not have been as effective in prose. As you read the following poems, what appeals to you? The playful language of the first one? The humor of the second? The poignancy of the next three? The imagery of the last two?

POETRY

Say Cheese
by Edie Lipinski

Welcome to the Cheese Shop, please come in and try some cheese!

We have English Farmhouse Cheddar and several brands of Bries.

Our goats include a Midnight Moon or try the Bucheron,

Perhaps you're fond of triple creams, then take some Seal Bay home.

Treat your taste buds to a wedge of moldy Maytag Blue,

Or buy some nutty Emmental to make a smooth fondue.

You must try our fresh Manchego from the sheep that live in Spain,

Or a creamy, soft Havarti one created by a Dane.

Before you go you must not miss a slice of Swiss Tonneau,

From Italy we offer Mozzarella Buffalo.

We have a fine red Leicester and a creamy Gormandise,

You see this is the place to shop when in the mood for cheese.

Here's our Asiago Stella and ripe Explorateur,

Let me offer you some Gouda as you're headed out the door.

And remember when you're hungry and you need a healthy snack,

We have several dozen cheeses you can try when you come back.

April Fool's Day
by Irene Hannigan

Like clockwork the roses arrive
each year one more than the last
to mark an April Fool's day event
first celebrated with a single-stem
sheepishly delivered
to my family's backdoor.
How sweet, said my mother.
What a boyfriend! exclaimed my sister.
What's the meaning of this? asked my father.

At college the roses still came,
but now phone calls casually timed
coinciding with the anticipated delivery.

Will this go on forever? my mother asked.
Must be costing a fortune! my sister said.
What's the meaning of all this? my father insisted.

And now there are fifty.

I lose myself in this year's gathering of
buds, blooms, stems, and thorns,
I clip, place, arrange and see
blurred snapshots and vignettes
that each one brings into focus.

So grateful am I for what I know
will not always be.

Awakening
by Mary Yardley

I love to swim
I love how the water
holds me
but doesn't constrain me.
I love how the knot
that lives in my gut
unwinds,
melting with every stroke.
and how
a strength
that normally sleeps deep inside
awakens.

Journey
by Martha Regan

Martha
the one who did what was expected
the one who caused no waves

Marty, Marcy, Marth
the one who was responsible
the one who caused no waves

Mrs. Michael Regan
the one who tended hearth and home
the one who caused no waves

Mummy, mumma, mother
the one who cared and nourished
the one who caused no waves

Thunder heard, the storm was near
She felt it in her bones
He up and left, now who was she?
She thought she caused no waves.
To hell with this, she took a risk
And stormed to Mexico
She learned to live to please herself
And created many waves.

Now Nana, Grammy, Grama
the one who lives to love and play
the one who jumps in waves.

Those
by Joan Stein

There are those
Who find friends easily,
Like sinking into down beds.
They loll, roll,
Touch fingers, toes,
intertwine, become two,
Then more.
Grow like honeycombs
Linking together,
Floating like hot air,
In balloons,
On top of the world.

And there are those
Who do not.
They lie on stones.
Feel everything.
Move painfully or
Not at all.
It is hard to touch
Or link bodies
Rolling on stone.
They are the cold air
Near to the ground.
Knowing it.
Feeling it.
Every rock and rill.
Becoming
Poets.

Snapshots from Spring 2014
by Penny Staples

I

How can blue be the color of depression?
In the monochrome of this never-ending winter,
the blue of the sky is the only thing that lifts the spirit,
and when a bluebird zigzags near,
the cerulean of its back catches the sun,
igniting joy.

II

Black hole in a wintry tree—
when shaded brown,

like an eyelid lowered,
the screech owl is home.

III

A fingernail clipping that missed the trash
has somehow been transported into the sky—
lunar apotheosis.

IV

Sometimes when you go looking for herons,
you find an owl instead—
pale pellets on the forest floor,
indigestible conglomerates of bone and fur,
like signs that say "Look up!"
A lumpy pyramid of feathers on a branch looks down—
baby great horned owl.

V

Amphibious symphony —
frogs peep, toads trill.
No need for a conductor.

VI

On the way to Wachusett, the car begins to weave
as Charlie cranes his neck to see out my window.
In my wifely role as corrector of husbandly inattention,
I harrumph and—pointedly—point ahead.
But he is so persistent in his off-road peer,
I look to the right and see the bird that is flapping alongside my window.
"Yes. It's a bald eagle," I sigh.
No more needed to be said.
We laugh at the marital moment.

VII

Streams run down every trail.
Bubbles like pearls race through clefts of rock,
collecting like frog spawn in the lulls of the downward rollick.

VIII

Yellow trumpets with leaves a motley hybrid of green and mauve,
a flower I do not see in the woods at home.
Out of my cache of jumbled memories,
the name comes to me effortlessly and unbidden,
small miracle in this age of creeping aphasia—
Trout lilies.

IX

Surprising me with his poetry,
my husband calls attention to
a "riot of roots" along the trail.
"Nice phrase," I say.

X

The tyranny of the to-do list—
we do not so much *pay* attention
as liberate it.

Helpless
by Irene Hannigan

> Only a lamppost
> remains
> at the street's edge
> where the white Cape
> with black shutters
> and red door has been
> for generations.
>
> Every single maple and pine—
> chopped, hacked, severed, split,
> enlarging the parcel of land
> that was big enough
> for so long
> for so many.
>
> The backhoe's jaws
> crunch the shingles,
> bash in the windows,
> crumble the foundation,
> devour the bricks
> of the latest victim
> as I wait for the epidemic
> to spread to the
> house across the street
> that is
> FOR SALE.

The following pieces of writing are all longer forms. Some began as a kernel of an idea in a word photo or journal entry, but were transformed into an anecdote or vignette. They illustrate how each writer experimented with techniques discussed in chapter six. Which ones capture your attention? Does the title draw you in? What about the lead sentence? Does the dialogue sound authentic? What words, phrases, and sentences are particularly appealing and why? Which ones pack an emotional punch that resonates with you?

ANECDOTES

Letting Go
by Mary Yardley

One sunny Monday afternoon last September my dog Sparky and I went for a walk in the woods. I remember thinking how fortunate I was— Lucky that I had my beautiful daughter, Samantha even if she had just left for college; lucky that I had good friends and my family; lucky that I had my dear dog, Sparky. Sam often teased me, "Sparky is not *your* dog, Mom. He's *our* dog."

The very next day, Sparky died. When I opened the front door something felt wrong. It wasn't that Sam was not there for I was getting used to that. It was too quiet. Usually Sparky came clamoring down the steps to greet me, his nails clicking on the wooden steps. But there was only silence. Then as I moved toward the kitchen, I saw him lying down right by the basement door so still that he looked like he was sleeping.

"Sparky!" I wailed, "Nooo!"

I scooped him up. His body was warm—perhaps he was only unconscious I thought. How I managed to grab my purse, get out the front door, the screen door, lock the front door and open the car door all with eighteen pounds sprawled over my arms, I do not know.

I nearly flew into Animal Emergency Care. "Help me," I called out. "You have to help my dog. He won't wake up." The vet exchanged a look with the police officer who had escorted my car. Later I knew what that look meant but I couldn't see it then.

As the vet took Sparky into another room I held myself tight, rocking on the chair in the waiting room, whispering. "No, Sparky please don't go now. Sam just left. Not now, Sparky."

When the vet returned he said, "I'm sorry. We did everything we could. You should know that whatever it was, it was quick." I asked to see him.

The nurse wheeled Sparky in on a table with a blanket carefully tucked around him. A corner was folded to make a pillow on which his head was resting. I rested my head on his thick, bouncy fur. I clung to him. How would I ever be able to let him go?

As I hugged him, sobbing, I felt my cell phone vibrate in my back pocket. I checked the caller ID. It was Sam; but I didn't pick up. I wasn't ready to tell her. I needed to keep her safe from our loss for a little longer.

Later that night after I returned home after having buried Sparky in a corner of my sister's wooded backyard I walked into the kitchen. There on the floor, where I had found Sparky hours before, lay a single rose petal.

How To Eat an English Muffin
by Eileen Nicole Simon

My oldest son, Anders, is autistic. He could not attend public school because he could not speak. That was before the special education law was passed. Instead my son was admitted to a weekday residential program at the old Massachusetts Mental Health Center, Ward 6. Weekends the children came home, from Friday afternoon until Sunday evening.

After picking Anders up from Ward 6 one Friday, we went to the supermarket. As we went down the bread aisle, Anders grabbed a package of *Thomas's English Muffins*.

"Okay, you want English muffins?" I asked.

"Yes," he replied.

Anders was now beginning to speak.

He also was learning a lot of useful things that went beyond being able to talk. He was observing and imitating things that the staff and other children did. He no longer isolated himself from other people. He was participating more and more in ward activities.

On Saturday morning I toasted an English muffin for Anders. I put a pat of butter on each slice and started to spread it.

"No, no, no!" he cried out.

Anders put the slices together and began to eat around the edge of the muffin. Then he opened up his muffin sandwich and continued eating along the edges of each half. Finally he got to the "dessert," the melted pat of butter at the center of each slice.

"I like to save the best for last," he said.

Discovery
by Martha Regan

"And next on our program this evening I would like to introduce Martha Hill, President of the National Honor Society," the emcee for the evening announced.

I slid out of my seat in the auditorium and walked quickly up the side steps of the stage to the podium and microphone in the center of the stage. I looked up and could see nothing but a blackened auditorium through the glaring lights. I took a deep breath and began my speech. But as I began to talk, I could hear my own words as if someone else was saying them.

"Ladies and Gentlemen I feel honored to be here tonight to talk about the National Honor Society."

As I started to talk about the qualifications for membership, I got caught up listening to my own words. Somehow I forgot that I was the speaker and it took me a few seconds to notice that suddenly I wasn't saying anything. I had instead become the audience and was listening to silence. While I knew the audience was waiting, I was mesmerized by my own mind and thoughts. It was as if I was taking pleasure in observing myself surviving without fear, the fact that I was on stage with an audience watching me forget my own message. In those few moments I felt a rush of excitement about that discovery until a friend in one of the front rows cued me as to what I was to say next.

I snapped out of my dream state and completed the speech without a hitch. This survival mechanism, however, continues to work for me in stressful situations. I have the capacity to step outside of myself so as not to feel fear in the actual situation.

Strand of Pearls
by Kristen Gobiel

I was nineteen when Gaga, my eighty-seven year old great-grandmother, needed to move into a nursing home. She had invited me to the studio apartment that she had called home for the past three years to help her finish packing. After having dinner together, we proceeded to pack her remaining personal items, which were few in number having downsized a number of times over the years to make her life simpler. She had always told me that physical possessions held little value for her.

When we were ready to go to sleep, I turned down the covers of the double bed while she busied herself in her vanity drawer. When she approached the bed, she handed me a small box.

"Something for you," she said quietly and then added, before I had a chance to say a word, "I want you to have these." I opened the box and inside was a strand of pearls, which I had seen her wear on special occasions— a gift from my grandfather.

"But I can't take them, Gaga," I said before adding, "You'll have many occasions left to wear them." But she knew better as she turned off the light and reached for my hand.

As we lay there in that bed, I never realized how small it was. I had lain in that bed since I was a young child, for countless sleepovers, always amazed at how big it was. Now for the first time I faced the reality that GaGa would not always be a part of my life. Our roles had reversed. She was now the frail one who needed her hand held in the darkness.

Her strand of pearls will always be my most valuable piece of jewelry. I wore them to her funeral. I wore them on my wedding day and every special occasion since then. They will always be the last physical representation of who my great-grandmother was. All of her independence, dignity and spirit were in those pearls that night she handed them to me. That's how she wanted me to remember her and she succeeded. My memories of her last few years in the nursing home are faint in comparison to that night. She was mistaken to believe that her life couldn't be captured in an object.

The Girl in the Yellow Coat
by Polly Attwood

The girl in the yellow coat stood motionless at the entrance to the street, trying desperately to ignore the dirt and squalor, to remember and believe that she had lived here once. Watching the faces for traces of friendly interest, or at least curiosity; but the blank eyes stared through her, grip shifting on greasy carrier bags, heavy bodies pressing the life out of weary feet, pushing, heedless through debris from the nearby marketplace. Surely, the children would be the same as she remembered?

As if in answer, a dark-skinned child ran screaming into the road, hotly pursued by four other children, pink with the effort of throwing mud and tin cans. Dispirited, the girl stared past the over-flowing dustbins to a line of depressed, grey nappies. A door slammed and an unseen voice yelled disinterested abuse.

A thin, wary tabby cat was watching her from the protection of a doorway. A brief ray of sun shone on the slow-drying puddles and caused the girl to move a few steps towards the cat, calling softly to it. Surprised and suspicious, it advanced a few steps and stopped. She paused as the cat did. The children, tired of waiting for their taunts to be answered, slung a tin can at the cat, which vanished, spitting, down the street.

The girl watched for a few seconds, and then turned and walked away. The sun, like the girl, gave up the unequal struggle, and disappeared behind the clouds.

A Memory of My Father
by Edie Lipinski

"In the name of the Father..." Avoiding my mother's disapproving look I inched forward until my feet touched the carpet, the red velvet cushion sliding with me.

"and of the Son..." I reached for the oblong piece of wood that held the pew door closed.

"and of the Holy Ghost..." Pulling the handle toward me I turned the latch.

"May the peace that passeth all understanding be with you now and remain with you forevermore..."

My patent leather shoes toed the line between aisle and pew. For more than an hour I had dwelt in the house of the Lord. I had used every crayon in the box to color Joseph's coat. I had looked up the date of Easter in 1979 and tried to imagine what on earth I would be doing in that impossibly far off year. I had let the wild cherry lifesaver melt ever so slowly on my tongue until it was wafer thin. The time for action was at hand.

"Amen."

The acolyte snuffed the candles. Before the silence dissolved into the rustle of women reaching for the purses, men standing to stretch and children rousing for sleep, I was across the main aisle and past the lectern. Opening the door silently I slipped in unnoticed. The smell of hair spray and cigar smoke filled the air. The crowded choir room was dimly lit and as my eyes adjusted to the light, I scanned the floor. I spotted the black wingtips and launched myself through the flurry of black and white robes. A gray flannel pant leg appeared and in an instant my arms were locked tight around my father's leg.

He was very tall and sang with the most beautiful tenor voice. Taking four steps to his one I maintained my grasp until he had hung up his gown, slipped on his navy topcoat and reached for his gray homburg hat. Finally his hand reached down to me. My father's fingers were exceptionally long (the long fingers my son would inherit) and my white-gloved hand disappeared inside his.

The church had been old when he sang there as a boy. Now it is historic. The heavy wooden door swung open on thick black hinges. We walked out into the sunshine. The congregation hurried home or stood in groups talking. Some children played tag in the graveyard. I stood by my father's side...content.

Books and Roses
by Gemma Munoz

In Catalonia, Saint George's Day on April 23 is one of the most beautiful days of the year. On that day the main street of all the towns are crowded and full of stands of books and roses. Men and women exchange these items to commemorate the legend of our patron saint— the story of a soldier who killed a dragon to save a princess from being sacrificed. From the dragon's blood sprouted a rose, which Saint George gave to the princess as a sign of love. Reflecting on the Saint George's Days of my life, I can tell a lot about myself.

As a child I used to go out with my mum for a walk to the town's main square where I always chose a book. We then visited my aunt and uncle's flower shop. They always told me, "When you grow up, you will come to help us, right?" When my father arrived home from work later that day he would always bring a rose for my mum and me, usually in different colors. Some years, even my brother got us roses.

Although it was nice to get flowers from my dad or brother I dreamt of the day I would get a rose from a boyfriend. But the one year I thought it might happen, my boyfriend decided to split up with me that very morning of Saint George's Day. No rose and no book.

Then I have a great memory of the festival during my college years as I helped my aunt and uncle in their flower shop. The first boy, who I really fell in love with, was studying in Italy but he ordered the flower at my uncle's shop and I got it as soon as I arrived in the morning! I spent the whole day floating on air as I made my deliveries to others.

And this made me think that it is probably my destiny to always be away from my loved one on Saint George's Day. Even when I married my husband Albert, business trips for one or the other of us always interfered for at least half of our festivals.

My most recent memory of Saint George's Day came along with the premature arrival of our twin girls, Abril and Nuria. Flowers were not allowed in the nursery but Albert got each of them their first rose by printing it out on a piece of paper and attaching it to their cribs. At least we were all together. That Saint George's Day was both the nicest and the hardest day ever proving to me how the ups and downs in my life will forever be reflected on that day.

Senior Portraits
by Richard Trakimas

Walking toward my first writers' class on the Tuft's campus I could not help but flash back to my own college days so many decades ago. As I passed the school bulletin board in the cafeteria a posted notice caught my eye. In bright blue letters it read—"Senior Portraits" listing the sign up steps to get on the photographer's schedule. I thought to myself—*Isn't that nice, they take portraits of the senior citizens attending the Osher LLI program!* I took a few steps and then it hit me. This notice wasn't about senior citizens—it was about actual senior year college students about to enter the REAL WORLD for the first time!

I struggled to understand how I could have made such a mistake. Was I being self-centered by thinking that, of course, the notice was about me, the senior citizen, or was it a case of a momentary flash back and that I was one with the students sitting in the student lounge studying their art history and marketing principles and Facebook?

It is hard to believe that so much of the world has changed in those decades since I graduated from college. It is as though I was a visitor from another planet, like the hovering fetus in the original *2001: A Space Odyssey* movie looking down at the world, observing rapid fire images from my life and the events going on around them. All the while remaining physically unchanged – ageless while the world aged.

Writing for the class dredges up memories from early childhood, a few more memories from high school, even a snippet or two from college. Why is it that the most distant memories are the most vivid? It is as if my brain is clouding from the outside in – the most recent memories are the toughest to hold on to. What was the joke I heard on TV last night that I wanted to share with friends today? What was it again that my wife asked me to pick up at the market today as she ran out the door to her job?

The ink of my life is fading and it will disappear entirely unless I do something about it. Everyone's stories are important, some are even interesting—like the time I was kidnapped in Korea while on a business trip. So I will write my stories to refresh my ink. Perhaps I will find enough segments to incorporate them into something larger. Perhaps someday a college will ask to have my senior citizen portrait taken.

Crumb Cakes
by Irene Hannigan

"You know, if I were an older woman who wanted to put butter on this muffin I wouldn't be able to," announced the old-enough woman at the counter at a local donut shop. She deliberately turned around to face the other regulars at the counter who were engaged in their scratch tickets or talking with friends while enjoying their mid-morning coffees and donuts.

"Look at it," she continued. "It just falls apart."

At that moment, Jerry, the owner emerged from the back room sensing that all was not right in his homey little establishment. He innocently inquired if there was something amiss.

"Well just look at this muffin," the woman explained. "Now I don't usually put butter on my muffins, which is a good thing. BUT, if I did, buttering this muffin would be impossible." With that she demonstrated the futility of the situation. The muffin, which was cradled in her palm, was in pieces.

"But it's a crumb cake," Jerry calmly but authoritatively stated, "and crumb cakes are just like that. Perhaps you don't really like crumb cakes."

"Oh, no I like them very much," she insisted.

Jerry turned, hiding a smile, "Well maybe it's a good thing you can't put butter on them, then. It makes them a rather healthy kind of muffin, don't you think?"

And with that a counter full of satisfied customers nodded their heads in agreement anxious to get back to their mid-morning routines. The woman however was determined to retake center stage as she had now finished her crumb cake-muffin.

"By the way," she inquired of Jerry. "When are you going to get the bus 80 schedules? You know, you have all the others over there." She waved her ringed index finger in the direction of the rack of bus schedules kept just beyond the counter of donuts.

Jerry took a deep breath and explained. "They send us some of all the schedules but you're right— that one seems to be out. You see, lots of people probably take more than one and so we run out." Jerry had hit the nail right on the head as the woman admitted to having taken two herself on occasion.

"Well, there you have it. That's why we run out."

"Oh, but I never throw them out. I take two just in case I lose one."

"And have you ever lost one?"

"Well no; but, how do I know when I will?"

With a twinkle in his eye, he said, "Well, dear, maybe you should just bring one back tomorrow and we'll hold it for you."

What a perfect answer for, to be sure, the woman would be back tomorrow right on schedule. Even though she couldn't butter the crumb cakes, they were still tasty. More importantly, though, a stop at Jerry's shop was always worth the trip before catching bus 80 to wherever she was heading.

Finding Inspiration from the Writing of Others

1. What writing pieces resonated with you in terms of their content?

Are you attracted to writings that are based on everyday occurrences or past memories? Do you appreciate the humor of some and the poignancy of others? Which pieces evoke a memory that reminds you of one of yours?

2. What forms appeal to you?

Are you attracted to shorter, more manageable word photos and writer's notebook entries? Even a short entry can be powerful. Are the poems appealing to you because they capture the essence of an experience? Are the anecdotes tempting to try because you like the idea of telling a longer story?

3. What have you learned about the authors?

Did you hear the author's voice come through in the words they wrote? Are you looking forward to noticing when your voice emerges from the words you produce? Do you think your writing will be humorous? Will it include dialogue? Will it be poetic? Are you curious about how it will evolve over time?

4. Would you like to keep in touch with me?

I would love to know what aspects of this book you've found useful. I'd be interested in learning where your writing has taken you. If you happen to live in my home state of Massachusetts, we might be able to get together. If not, an email (ihannigan50@gmail.com) is another option. I hope that writing becomes a pleasurable pastime and that you *make* time to write on!

163

Bibliography

Beckham, Beverly. *A Gift of Time.* Lexington, Kentucky: Host Creative Communications, 1991.

Beckham, Beverly. *Back Then.* Lexington, Kentucky: Host Creative Communications, 2000.

Beckham, Beverly. "When Your Memory is Merely Jogging in Place." *The Boston Globe*, Nov. 5, 2006.

Berg, Elizabeth. *Escaping into the Open: The Art of Writing True.* New York: Harper Collins, 1999.

Clarke, Roy Peter. *Writing Tools.* New York: Little, Brown and Company, 2006.

Elbow, Peter. *Writing With Power: Techniques for Mastering the Writing Process.* New York: Oxford University Press, 1981.

Fletcher, Ralph. *Breathing In, Breathing Out: Keeping a Writer's Notebook.* Portsmouth, NH: Heinemann, 1996.

Goldberg, Natalie. *Writing Down the Bones: Freeing the Writer Within.* Boston: Shambhala Publications, 2005.

Gould, June. *The Writer in All of Us: Improving Your Writing Through Childhood Memories.* New York: Plume, 1991.

Hannigan, Irene. *Off to School: A Parent's-Eye View of the Kindergarten Year.* Washington, DC: National Association for the Education of Young Children, 1998.

Hannigan, Irene. *A Principal's Journey: The School as My Classroom.* Waltham, MA: Boston Writers Publishing, 2014.

Hannigan, Irene. "What a Way to Be." Lexington, MA: *Lexington Life Times*, 2018.

Heard, Georgia. *Writing Toward Home: Tales and Lessons to Find Your Way.* Portsmouth, NH: Heinemann, 1995.

Kidder, Tracy and Richard Ford. *Good Prose: The Art of Nonfiction.* New York: Random House, 2013.

King, Stephen. *On Writing: A Memoir.* New York: Simon & Schuster, 2000.

Lamott, Anne. *Bird by Bird: Some Instructions on Writing and Life.* New York: Pantheon, 1994.

Lapate, Phillip. *To Show and To Tell: The Craft of Literary Nonfiction.* New York: Free Press, 2013.

MacLachlan, Patricia. *Journey.* New York: Bantam Doubleday, 1991.

Moore, Dinty W. *The Mindful Writer.* Somerville, MA: Wisdom Publications, 2016.

Murray, Donald. *Crafting a Life in Essay, Story, Poem.* Portsmouth, NH: Boynton/Cook Publishers, 1996.

Murray, Donald. *My Twice-Lived Life: A Memoir.* New York: Ballantine Books, 2001.

Murray, Donald. *Writing for Your Readers.* Chester, CT: The Globe Pequot Press, 1983.

Murray, Donald. "Living Life Again Through Writing." *The Boston Globe,* June 25, 2002.

Murray, Donald. "Writing Should Be a Voyage of Discovery." *The Boston Globe,* October 25, 2005.

Schneider, Pat. *Writing Alone and With Others.* New York: Oxford University Press, 2003.

Shapiro, Dani. *Still Writing: The Perils and Pleasures of a Creative Life.* New York: Grove Press, 2013.

Strunk, William and E.B. White. *The Elements of Style.* New York: Macmillan Publishing Co., 1979.

Theroux, Phyllis. *The Journal Keeper: A Memoir.* New York: Atlantic Monthly Press, 2010.

Zinsser, William. *On Writing Well.* New York: Harper Collins, 1990.

PERMISSIONS

I am grateful to the following publishers for permission to use the quotes that precede chapters one, four, five, six, and seven.

WRITING WITH POWER by Elbow (1981) 21w from p.13 to be used as an epigraph ©1981 by Oxford University Press. By permission of Oxford University Press, USA.

Excerpt from BIRD BY BIRD: SOME INSTRUCTIONS ON WRITING AND LIFE by Anne Lamott, copyright © 1994 Anne Lamott. Used by permission of Pantheon Books, an imprint of the Knopf Doubleday Publishing Group, a division of Penguin Random House LLC. All rights reserved.

Adapted from *The Art of Teaching Writing* by Lucy McCormick Calkins, Copyright © 1986, 1994 by Lucy McCormick Calkins. Published by Heinemann.

From *Writing Toward Home: Tales and Lessons to Find Your Way* by Georgia Heard. Copyright © 1995 by Georgia Heard. Published by Heinemann.

Crafting a Life in Essay, Story, Poem by Donald Murray, ©1996 by Heinemann, Reprinted by permission of The Rosenberg Group of behalf of the Author's estate.

Many thanks to the following individuals who agreed to have their writing appear in Chapter 8 and Chapter 10:

Polly Attwood	*The Girl in the Yellow Coat*
Polly Attwood	*Uncle Cecil*
Carol Birdsall	*Dear Fifth Grade Teacher*
Sandra S. Bittenbender	*What More Could I Ask For?*
Jenn Eisenheim	*Lost and Found*
Kristen Gobiel	*Strand of Pearls*
Margaret Gooch	*Brightening Up a Gray Day*
Tim Harrington	*An Unforgettable Adventure*
Annette Hodess	*Always Drink Scotch*
Joe Johnston	*Morning Coffee*
Judy B. Katz	*A Virtual Tour of Life*
Edie Lipinski	*Say Cheese*
Edie Lipinski	*A Memory of My Father*
Edie Lipinski	*Found Food*
Edie Lipinski	*Letter to Writing Group*
Gemma Munoz	*Books and Roses*
Martha Regan	*Journey*

Irene Hannigan never leaves home without a little notebook tucked into the pocket of whatever she is wearing. As a parent, teacher, staff developer, and principal writing has always been an important part of her daily routine. She currently offers workshops and courses to adults who are interested in using writing as a tool for their own personal and professional growth. She is the author of *A Principal's Journey: The School as My Classroom, Off to School: A Parent's-Eye View of the Kindergarten Year* as well as many articles about education.

Laura Schreiber is a professional designer, illustrator, and award-winning watercolorist who never leaves home without *her* little sketch notebook tucked into her pocket. Her love for sketching began in seventh grade as an art class assignment and continues to this day. She works in her log cabin studio in northern New Jersey.

Made in the USA
Lexington, KY
13 September 2018